My Self, My Muse

Sanford Sternlicht, *Series Editor*

My Self, My Muse

Irish Women Poets
Reflect on Life and Art

Edited by
Patricia Boyle Haberstroh

SYRACUSE UNIVERSITY PRESS

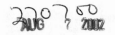

Library of Congress Cataloging-in-Publication Data

My self, my muse : Irish women poets reflect on life and art / edited by Patricia Boyle
Haberstroh.—1st ed.

    p. cm—(Irish studies)

    Includes bibliographical references and index.

    ISBN 0-8156-2909-5 (cloth : alk. Paper)—ISBN 0-8156-2910-9 (pbk. : alk. paper)

    1. Women poets, Irish—Biography. 2. English poetry—Women authors—History and
criticism—Theory, etc. 3. English poetry—Irish authors—History and criticism—Theory,
etc. 4. Irish poetry—Women authors—History and criticism—Theory, etc. 5. Women and
literature—Ireland—History—20th century. 6. Poets, Irish—20th century—Biography. 7.
Creation (literary, artistic, etc.) 8. Ireland—In literature. 9. Poetry—Authorship. I.
Haberstroh, Patricia Boyle. II. Irish studies (Syracuse, N.Y.)

PR8733.M9 2001

821'.91099287'09417—dc21   00-068772

For my mother and father
Born in Donegal

Contents

Illustrations

Contributors

Eavan Boland is the author of eight volumes of poetry, including *Outside History: Selected Poems 1980–1990, An Origin Like Water: Collected Poems 1967–87,* and *Selected Poems: 1989.* Her two most recent volumes are *In a Time of Violence* (1994) and *The Lost Land* (1998). She has also published a volume of essays, *Object Lessons: The Life of the Woman and the Poet in Our Time.* She is Melvin and Bill Lane Professor in Humanities at Stanford University and has won awards from the Lannan Foundation and the American Ireland Fund.

Catherine Byron was raised in Belfast, the child of a Galway mother and an English father. After study at Oxford, she farmed in the west of Scotland, and she now lives in central England, where she teaches at Nottingham Trent University. Her first collection, *Settlements,* was published in 1985; *Fat-Hen Field Hospital* appeared in 1993 and *The Getting of Vellum* in 2000. She is also the author of a prose work, *Out of Step, Pursuing Seamus Heaney to Purgatory* (1992).

Moya Cannon, born in Donegal, now lives in Galway, where she has spent several years teaching adolescent travelers. Her first collection, *Oar,* won the Brendan Behan Memorial Prize in 1991; her second collection, *The Parchment Boat,* was published in 1997. She has been a writer-in-residence at universities in both Canada and Ireland.

Patricia Boyle Haberstroh is professor of English at La Salle University in Philadelphia. She has served as Women's Studies Editor for *New Hibernia Review* and on the Editorial Board of *Nua: Studies in Contemporary Irish Writ-*

ing. Her book, *Women Creating Women, Contemporary Irish Women Poets* (1996), won the Donald Murphy Award given by the American Conference for Irish Studies and was selected by *Choice* as one of the outstanding books published in the United States in 1996.

Medbh McGuckian has published six major collections of poetry, including *Marconi's Cottage* (1991), *Captain Lavender* (1994), and *Shelmalier* (1998); she has also published her *Selected Poems* (1997). McGuckian has received the Alice Hunt Bartlett Prize, the Bass Ireland Award for Literature, and the Cheltenham Award. She lives in Belfast and teaches in the creative writing program at Queen's University in Belfast.

Joan Newmann, born in County Armagh, graduated from Queen's University in Belfast and lived for many years in Ballycastle. She now resides in Donegal. She has been writer-in-residence at the Verbal Arts Centre in Derry and an active member of the Word of Mouth Creative Writing Collective. Her first collection, *Coming of Age,* was published in 1995; a chapbook, *Thin Ice,* appeared in 1998.

Eiléan Ní Chuilleanáin has published six volumes of poetry, including *The Second Voyage* (1986), *The Magdalene Sermon* (1989), and *The Brazen Serpent* (1995). Winner of both the Irish Times Award for poetry and the Patrick Kavanagh Award, she is also the editor of a collection of essays, *Irish Women: Image and Achievement* (1985). A Fellow of Trinity College Dublin, she lives in Dublin.

Nuala Ní Dhomhnaill, born in Lancashire and raised in the west of Ireland, writes poetry only in Irish; many of Ireland's well-known poets have translated her work for bilingual editions. Her three collections in Irish are *An Dealg Droighin* (1981), *Féar Suaithinseach* (1984), and *Feis* (1991). Bilingual volumes include *Selected Poems/Rogha Dánta* (1993; translations by Michael Hartnett), *Pharaoh's Daughter* (1990; various translators), and *The Astrakhan Cloak* (1992; translations by Paul Muldoon). She has won both the Seán Ó Ríordáin Award and the Arts Council Prize for Poetry and lives in Dublin.

Mary O'Malley has published five collections of poetry, including *A Consideration of Silk* (1990), *Where the Rocks Float* (1993), *The Knife in the Wave*

(1997), and *Asylum Road* (2001), and has edited two books of children's writing. She has lived in London and Portugal and currently resides in the Moycullen Gaeltacht in Galway. She was elected to Aosdána, a government-sponsored arts organization, and has been writer-in-residence in Derry and Mayo.

Eithne Strong, a poet in both Irish and English, and a fiction writer, died in 1999. Among her fifteen books are five collections of poetry in Irish and six collections in English, including *Flesh . . . the Greatest Sin* (1980), *My Darling Neighbour* (1985), *Let Live* (1990), and a volume of selected poems, *Spatial Nosing* (1993). She also wrote two novels and a collection of short stories. She lived in Dublin and was a member of Aosdána.

My Self, My Muse

Prologue

Not Your Muse

PAULA MEEHAN

I'm not your muse, not that creature
in the painting, with the beautiful body,
Venus on the half-shell. Can
you not see I'm an ordinary woman
tied to the moon's phases, bloody
six days in twenty-eight? Sure

I'd like to leave you in love's blindness,
cherish the comfort of your art, the way
it makes me whole and shining,
smooths the kinks of my habitual distress,
never mentions how I stumble into the day,
fucked up, penniless, on the verge of whining

at my lot. You'd have got away with it
once. In my twenties I often traded a bit
of sex for immortality. That's a joke.
Another line I swallowed, hook
and sinker. Look at you—
rapt, besotted. Not a gesture that's true

1

on that canvas, not a droopy breast,
wrinkle or stretchmark in sight.
But if it keeps you happy who am I
to charge in battledressed to force you test
your painted doll against a harsh light
I live by, against a brutal merciless sky.

(Meehan 1994, 24)

Introduction

PATRICIA BOYLE HABERSTROH

‿ A few years ago, at a reading by an Irish poet, I sat among a very diverse audience, ranging from some who often read Irish poetry to others who knew little about contemporary poetry and poets. In the middle of the reading, the poet stopped to try to convince us that his life was fairly ordinary; then he began to describe how he used some of the details of his own life in his poems. While I had hoped he would read more poems, other listeners were enchanted with this approach, and what started as a reading turned into a dialogue between the poet and his audience. This disruption of the structure of the traditional poetry reading, while initially disconcerting, opened my eyes once again to some of the attractions of poetry we can easily ignore. When the poet returned to read a few final poems, I was aware of the vast gap that sometimes exists between the experience of hearing or reading a poem and writing about poetry. Likewise, this reading reaffirmed for me the connections listeners and readers can make between a poet's life and work and, ultimately, between a poet's experiences and their own.

Reflecting on this event later, I thought about how recent discussions of poetry and poetic theory have sometimes made us suspicious of what occurred at that reading, especially as this concerns autobiographical details in any poem. In literary criticism, the relationship between a poet's life and work has been the center of controversy for over half a century. To illustrate, we could graph two points: at one, poetry has been read as confessional, where the boundary between life and poem is sometimes blurred; at the other, readers challenge the concept of any subjective voice, obliterating perceived links between poet and persona. Along the line between these points, numerous theories and movements have been plotted, many of which may influence how people write and read poems. Critics have debated questions of subjectivity and objectivity, impersonality, representation, language structures, unified subject, persona, and voice in a poem. Readers and critics have staked out territory with manifestos, terminology, and guidelines, defining what a poem is and how to approach it. Competing theories and theorists have suggested new, and often seemingly conflicting, ways to read a poem. In the midst of all this, poets go on writing poems.

These debates have occurred within the broad spectrum of the place of the poet both in his or her own culture and in a wider cultural framework, a point discussed by the audience and the poet at the reading I described above. If the relationship of the poet to a persona in a poem raises questions, even greater problems arise in considering the poem, the poet, and the reader in the context of the culture or cultures from which each emerged. And the term *culture* itself has been subjected to continual interpretation. From a narrow, time-bound, political or geographical meaning, *culture* has been redefined to include such aspects as race, class, gender, national identity, religion and sexual orientation. This new interpretation has led to considerations of majority and minority cultures, issues of colonization, and the impact of oppression on the expression of minority or indigenous people—considerations that underpin any discussion of "voice" in a poem.

All of these issues present convincing reasons for reconsidering the relationship between a poet's life and the expression of that in a poem. A fundamental issue in these discussions is, as Yeats always claimed, basically philosophical and aesthetic: it involves the transformation of some experience, whether we describe it as personal or cultural, into art. That transformation— what inspires it, what influences it, what controls it, how it happens—still has about it enough of the mysterious to warn us to be careful about putting too much faith in our ability to understand how a poem is written. Likewise, how a poem is read—what the reader constructs, recreates, accepts, rejects—involves both personal and communal meanings assimilated in numerous ways. When Keats wrote about negative capability or Eliot[1] about objective correlatives, both were trying to put a name to a process, to make the poem "imper-

---

1. Eliot is a good example of someone who tried too hard to see his work as separate from his life. Lyndall Gordon's biographies, *Eliot's Early Years* (1977) and *Eliot's New Life* (1988), illustrate very clearly the connections between Eliot's life and poems.

sonal," in Eliot's view. Nevertheless, events in the lives of each of these poets certainly find their way into their work.

At the same time, we can neither accept nor reject automatically the impact of a poet's own personal or cultural experience on the finished poem. Some readings of Sylvia Plath's poems provide a good example of how a tragic life can be used to distort both the meaning and evaluation of a poem. One certainly cannot appreciate the full value of the very successful poems of Plath's final year outside the context of her life (and how she described that life in prose), but the poems are more than autobiography, and we do a disservice to Plath to see her as what Eavan Boland has aptly described as "a character in an American melodrama" (1997, 22–25).

The creative process, where word, image, syntax, rhythm embody both idea and feeling, often reflects an experience that generated it, but the process of transformation is certainly not an easy one to describe. The psychology of creativity is still a very inexact science, and language has its own ability to subvert a writer's intention or a reader's response. On another level, however, when someone reads (or hears) a poem, part of the value of that poem may come from the expression of the experience described; images of loss generated by a writer's experience of loss, for example, carry feelings to which the reader responds. No doubt good poems have value even if a reader knows nothing about biographical or cultural context, but it is hard to deny that awareness of those contexts can add another, often significant, dimension to a poem.

The relationship between autobiographical experience, cultural constructs, and poetic voice has become increasingly important in Irish poetry, primarily because of the numerous approaches one can take to Irish culture and the Irish poem. Until recently, for example, when most readers defined the Irish poem, the context was male. However, gender has become an issue not only in Irish culture but also in the Irish poem. Much of this new emphasis can be attributed to the increasing visibility of talented Irish women writers and to the gap many of these women see between their own experiences and cultural constructions of Irish womanhood, Irish history, and Irish poetry. As the essays in this book reveal, much of what Irish women write about comes from the experiences of their daily lives as women and poets, experiences sometimes at odds with conventional images of Irish womanhood and Irish poetry. An awareness of a gendered cultural context, therefore, often enhances our understanding of a poem, especially when a woman poet challenges those images, either explicitly or implicitly.

On the broad issue of impersonality in a poem, gender presents a further complication. The American poet Carol Muske in her book, *Women and Poetry, Truth, Autobiography and the Shape of the Self,* suggests that women "may be just *too good* at negative capability, if we understand it as a kind of cultivated self-absence" (1997, 8). Often socialized to be passive and silent, or to avoid taboo subjects like female anatomy and sexuality, or devalued subjects like motherhood and children, women poets must confront and resist such gendering in order to examine and write about their own experience.

But assuming a subject position, or creating a female voice, has additional complications because women have often served as objects for the male poet. The muse, a conventional symbol of poetic inspiration, illustrates the problem. Traditionally female (and often "anatomically correct" according to some romanticized female image), the muse has played the role of intermediary for male poets, a source of inspiration, a helpmate in translating experience into art. In confronting the problem of this stereotyped figure, women poets must imagine themselves as both image and imagemaker,[2] subject and object, and reject gendered figures like the conventional muse. In effect, they often become their own muses, validating female experience as both starting point and subject of their literary work. In addressing this problem, poets like Medbh McGuckian and Nuala Ní Dhomhnaill have created ironic images of male muses, in poems that foreground female experience. These and other innovations have had a profound effect on the Irish poem in the emergence of more representative female voices and images.

Much has been written of the silent woman in literature and myth, of the female subordinated to the male hero, of the woman who serves as Other or muse for the male writer. Mary DeShazer argues that women writers often respond to this situation with specific strategies: "Rather than searching for an Other against whom to define the self, creative women turn first inward for sustenance to the multiple selves of their own psyches, then outward to the doubles and shadows reflected in other powerful women: mothers, sisters, lovers, muses—alternate selves interwoven by the common thread of female imagination and experience" (1986, 6–7). While some might, and indeed have argued against too much emphasis on a common, essential, female imag-

---

2. Eavan Boland has written frequently about this problem. See especially the essays in *Object Lessons, The Life of the Woman and the Poet in Our Time* (Boland 1995).

ination and experience, we can certainly trace the recurrence of shared experience and similar images in writing by women. The relationship of those images and experiences to a woman's voice and a woman's life is the subject of much of the material in this book. In her study *Clearing the Space: A Why of Writing,* the Irish poet and playwright Anne Le Marquand Hartigan maintains that "No one else can write in your voice" and that women must make a space, find their "place in the pattern" (1996, 14). The essays and memoirs that follow illustrate how women poets are doing this.

Transforming experience into poetry inevitably involves questions of identity. In Ireland those questions reverberate in many ways, and include gender identity. If one looks for a predominant idea in the pieces in this book, personal identity is a central theme and female identity a part of a larger construct of Irish identity. But the issue of female identity in Ireland is further complicated by the female icons embedded in Ireland's political troubles. As Lia Mills explains, "In Ireland, the familiar concept of the Muse as 'feminine' is further complicated by the symbolism of Mother Ireland, a relatively modern ideological construct of a Celtic figure." Describing the evolution of this figure from triple goddess to dream woman (the *spéirbhean* or *aisling*) who inspired Gaelic poets, Mills shows how in the nineteenth century the *Shean Bhean Bhoct* (Poor Old Woman/Mother Ireland) became "a source of inspiration, a call to arms for patriots, and an image that "became sanctified in the genesis of the new republic." Noting that Celtic mythology provided other active and independent female figures, Mills also suggests that none of these "fitted comfortably within a modern agenda that defined the family rather than the individual as the unit of society and recorded in its constitution that a woman's place should be in the home" (1995, 73–74). In Mills's view, contemporary Irish women, primarily poets, are challenging this iconic female by "establishing a dialogue between the mythical and the real in the context of the lived experience of women in Ireland" (1995, 69).

∽

At the beginning of her essay in this book, Nuala Ní Dhomhnaill addresses the issue of individual identity by recalling a childhood memory in which someone once asked her: "Cé leis tú?" [Who do you belong to?]. Noting that she brought herself "bristling" up to the height of "three foot nothing," Ní Dhomhnaill recalls how she replied: "Ní le héinne mé. Is liom féin mé féin" [I don't belong to anyone. I belong to myself]. This subject of belonging, of possession and its counterpart dispossession, runs like a river through much of contemporary Irish culture and literature, its streams meandering through geography, politics, race, language, religion, and, for women writers especially, gender.

The cultural construction of Irish womanhood, supported by state and church, and built on a firm foundation of life at home as wife and mother, each of the women poets writing for this book, using her own life as an example, has addressed in a different way. Ní Dhomhnaill's essay, it seems to me, makes clear how difficult it can be to "belong to oneself" in Ireland. In her poem "In Memoriam Elly Ní Dhomhnaill (1884–1963)," which precedes the essay, the poet celebrates an aunt, an educated, unmarried woman who struggled to establish an individual identity within her family and church, a "proud spirit, / who had no call to lie / with a man her match." An honors graduate in biology, Elly Ní Dhomhnaill challenged the stereotypes of Irish womanhood, trying to define a life for herself beyond the boundaries defined by Irish culture.

But as Nuala Ní Dhomhnaill, who writes in the Irish language, explains, the issue of who one belongs to includes questions not only of gender but also of language and politics, and the interaction between all of these complicates the issue of individual identity. Describing her own relationship with West Kerry, Ní Dhomhnaill says, *"of* the Gaeltacht, I am not *from* the Gaeltacht," illustrating the difficulty of writing in a displaced language. She makes it clear that the usurping of Irish by English is part of a larger displacement illustrated in emigration and the Diaspora. Language, like politics, like gender, constitutes one of several identifying and often interrelated markers Ní Dhomhnaill and the other women poets here address.

For the nine poets included in this book, the political conflicts within Ireland and between Ireland and England resonate differently, depending not only on where they have lived or are living, but also on the fact that they are women. Medbh McGuckian, Joan Newmann, and Catherine Byron, all raised in Northern Ireland, describe their own confusion about Irish identity. Noting that she never really learned her own history, Newmann describes studying "No Irish history—only what happened in other places." From her present vantage point in England, Byron sees Ireland through a different filter, and, as her essay demonstrates, her return for a pilgrimage on Station Island in Donegal marks an unexpected and ironic enlightenment about her own female Irish identity, an enlightenment that evolved into her poem "Coffin. Crypt. Consumption." Likewise, in the diary Medbh McGuckian kept at the end of the 1960s, one can see the tension between the evolving selves and identities of a young woman in a troubled land, embryonic forerunners of the numerous images of the self that later appear in McGuckian's poems. The conflicts faced by a developing woman and poet working in the midst of the political troubles in Belfast clearly emerge in McGuckian's work, making her poetry different from that written by men from Northern Ireland.

The Dublin-based poets, although removed from the daily battles McGuckian recounts, nonetheless record their own struggle with the concepts of political and national identity, often male-defined. Eithne Strong, who left Limerick at nineteen to settle in Dublin, recounts her family's resistance to, and her own reconciliation with, being "Married to the Enemy," the Englishman Rupert Strong. Her challenges to inherited images of Irish nationhood and Irish womanhood that came from family, school, and religion lie behind much of her poetry and the poetic persona of Mrs. Mahony, an important figure in several of Strong's poems.

Eavan Boland, directly addressing in her essay the image of the Irish woman poet within a national tradition, details her own attempts as a female to transcend the "restrictions and flawed permissions" of the male poem she inherited and the nationalist poem's construction of the Irish female. Boland celebrates the opening up of Irish poetry to "a precious addition of idiom and vista" and the reordering of the Irish poem that women poets have accomplished. Separating nation from nationalist, Boland recounts her struggle to find a place in a literature that she believes reduced woman to icon, and she discusses her challenge to the idea that she could be an Irish poet only if she sacrificed the right to explore her identity as a woman poet. In choosing an Irish icon for her poem "Anna Liffey," Boland revises the image of a traditional female figure named after a Dublin river and popularized in literature by male writers like Joyce. This revising she describes in her poem as "Usurping a name and a theme" (1994, 43).

On the west coast of Ireland, Moya Cannon and Mary O'Malley echo Ní Dhomhnaill's concerns about identity and belonging, though they both write poetry in English. O'Malley, "raised between languages" on the Connemara coast, describes herself as a "colonized child, linguistically speaking," inheriting her grandparents' Irish but raised speaking English. Nevertheless, as her essay shows, O'Malley feels strongly the pull of the deeper language that still underlies the oral and mythic traditions of rural Ireland. Like Ní Dhomhnaill, O'Malley rediscovers in these myths the female figures defined and subordinated by patriarchal forces; often, like Boland, she reinterprets these in terms of her own life experience. Cannon, raised in Donegal and living in Galway, meditates on the richness of the Irish language, which she has described in her poetry as Ireland's "mother" tongue. Despite its decreasing use, and all the political issues embedded in that loss, Cannon takes solace in Irish having survived "on the periphery of European history."

Whether expressed directly or indirectly, gender and gender politics play important roles in the poetry these women write, and their own personal experiences strongly influence their poems. Eavan Boland argues that recently Irish women poets "have disturbed certain traditional balances in the Irish poem between object and author, between poet and perspective." Boland also maintains that women poets are "influencing the form they enact." From the perspective of gender, the pieces that follow are most revealing as the poets illustrate how a person, event, or place generated a poem they wrote—how their own lives provided material for their poems.

In her essay, Eiléan Ní Chuilleanáin states: "A woman writer must have a female voice." But she also addresses questions which many of these poets have struggled with: "Does the voice come from the subject?" and "Was a female subject one which came merely from an assemblage of concerns that has been brushed into the corner labeled 'women'?" Ní Chuilleanáin's title, "Nuns: A Subject for a Woman Writer," leads us into an essay in which the poet's relationship with three aunts opens up to give us a broader picture of both the history of nuns and the history of Irish women. "My curiosity was drawn," Ní Chuilleanáin writes, "to the way their lives, their attention, were disciplined and directed to the physical world at all times, because it seemed a special case of the way women's lives had been lived." Alluding to the better known history of Irish women's lives, "the story of their confinement to home and maternity, of their defeat or marginalisation as workers, of Magdalens and typists, of mental patients, tuberculosis sufferers, of teachers and farmers," Ní Chuilleanáin suggests that the history of nuns "is no odder, surely, than the history of armies, which have been close to the center of almost every state that has ever existed." By explaining how her own experience with her aunts influenced poems like "J'ai Mal à nos Dents," Ní Chuilleanáin demonstrates both how personal experience can be recast in a poem and how the images in a poem embody broader meaning. By so doing, Ní Chuilleanáin is disturbing the "traditional balances" Boland alludes to and, in "enacting" her experience, also creating a female voice.

The confidence to see subjects from their daily lives as valid for poetry, or to see themselves as their own muse, is something many women poets have had to develop. Male literary voices loom large in most Irish women writers' early literary education and poetic development, and male writers were sometimes the only gauge against which they measured themselves. In the pieces that follow, the major names in modern Irish poetry, W. B. Yeats, Patrick Kavanagh, Louis MacNeice, John Montague, Seamus Heaney, crop up frequently. Interestingly, however, many of the allusions in these essays are to European and American female writers like Anna Ahkmatova, Denise Levertov, and Emily Dickinson, evidence perhaps that only recently have the women poets of Ireland's own past begun to receive the attention they deserve.

As the following pieces illustrate, awareness of themselves as women writers often involved a learning and a distancing process. Medbh McGuckian writes at one point in her diary that "Keats and I no longer see eye to eye," and Joan Newmann's valuable experience with the Group poets in Belfast is subtly qualified with her later observation: "Retrospectively, Denise Levertov and Adrienne Rich perhaps did not get as much attention as they deserved." Although ongoing research is uncovering the work of earlier Irish women writers, there is little evidence in this volume that these writers influenced the poets represented here—understandable, given that access to the work was, and is still, limited. Both Ní Chuilleanáin and Cannon allude to the poetry of Eibhlín Ní Chonaill, the best known Irish woman writer from the past; "Lament for Art O'Leary," an elegy for her dead husband, is popular throughout Ireland. While describing a slender line that connects women writing in the Irish language, Ní Chuilleanáin maintains, however, that an "Irish woman writing in the international void of English has to define herself in relation to a vital masculine tradition and to reach out to a rapidly developing movement of women's writing all over the world."

At the same time, challenges to the male domination of the Irish poetry landscape are clearly now in evidence. As her diary from when she was a student shows, McGuckian was already testing a female subject, style, and language. Hints of her later, gender-ambivalent and gender-challenging poetry carry overtones of role reversal as the young woman poet usurps the authority of the male: "John says English here is sterile," McGuckian writes in Northern Ireland, "maybe I will inseminate it." Embodying connotations of both national and gender politics, such entries foreshadow McGuckian's continual resistance to traditional literary, linguistic, and political authority and style, and to the male-defined English poem.

Gender issues are also at the heart of Catherine Byron's essay. Setting out to discover the "out of earshot" women she failed to find in Seamus Heaney's poem *Station Island* (1984), Byron eventually uncovered something quite unexpected in the ritual of fasting that the pilgrimage to Station Island demands. The silence about women, who make up the majority of pilgrims to the shrine, prompted Byron to confront something in herself: "the learned privileging of the male, so exquisitely inculcated in a Catholic girlhood in Ulster, and hardly shaken by years of being intellectually a feminist." Such confrontations are necessary, Patricia Coughlan maintains, because for some male poets "woman, the primary inhabitor and constituent of the domestic realm, is admiringly observed, centre stage but silent." Coughlan suggests that "What ostensibly offers itself as a celebration may be read as a form of limiting definition, in which certain traditional qualities of the feminine are required to persist for a fit wife, mother or Muse to come into being." Coughlan adds that the "constant naming of autobiographical 'originals' for these figures effectively masks this nearly ubiquitous blotting out of the individual qualities of *actual* women by the dominant—and stereotyped—ideal" (1991, 90). To avoid such stereotyping, one of Byron's stated purposes is to foreground the actual women who visit Station Island by writing about her own visit there.[3]

As Eithne Strong's essay shows, however, problems with religion were not restricted to Ulster nor, necessarily, to gender. Catholicism demanded that Strong's Protestant husband convert, something he could not do, and her subsequent forsaking of the Catholic Church for her own personal freedom led to a long and difficult separation from her family. From another angle, Moya Cannon, looking at the relationship between gender, politics, and religion, links some images of women to the interconnection of religion and a "heady romantic nationalism" underpinning an educational system where a woman's only role was as a "nurturer and facilitator."

For many of these poets, Christian tradition, embodied in the culture of both church and state, has created boundaries to challenge, a struggle that Cannon describes as overcoming a "passive acceptance" of dogma. Especially for the women raised in the Irish-speaking areas of rural Ireland, the sense of an older tradition alive in myths and legends has been a strong impetus for their writing. Nuala Ní Dhomhnaill's ability to connect the modern sense of

---

3. Byron has also written a full-length memoir of this visit entitled *Out of Step: Pursuing Seamus Heaney to Purgatory* (1992a).

the subconscious, for her the source of all creativity, with the mythic past has validated the pre-Christian Irish literary tradition for a modern world. Ní Dhomhnaill argues that the spoken word is a "plumbline into the subconscious" and that in Ireland "the door between the rational and irrational has never been locked tight shut." Moya Cannon sees similar psychological components in the older Irish nature lyric, and Mary O'Malley describes the influence of the rituals and local myths of Connemara on her poetry. In the work of all three of these poets, their life in the West has been transformed in many different ways into their work, and the emphasis on their own experience as the genesis of that transformation is clearly demonstrated.

The image of a living subject or a personal memory as the impetus for a creative act runs through the pieces in this book, in both poetry and prose, and is a testament to the influence of autobiography on the writing of poetry. But the process of metamorphosis is anything but neat and tidy. McGuckian's diary describes writing as "a lonely struggle with the mind"; Moya Cannon defines her poetry as making her way "out of some sort of chaos." McGuckian, alluding to Thomas Hardy's love poems, writes that she could not wear his "mask." The image of the mask through which the poet speaks is an old one, popularized in modernist and Irish poetry by Yeats, but Yeats's mask (or Hardy's), male masks, seem of little value for the woman poet. In her essay Mary O'Malley offers instead the image of the *sean nos* singer, a woman whose voice stirs in the listener great emotion while her face remains impassive, what O'Malley calls "a perfect mask." Agreeing with Seamus Heaney that the poet must move beyond autobiography, O'Malley also supports Eavan Boland's statement that "poetry enters where myth touches history," but this history must include women. The value of the *sean nos* singer for O'Malley comes from the fact that this is a female voice, a female mask, part of a female tradition.

For O'Malley, and for the other poets in this volume, the vehicle for transforming life into art is metaphor: "I am anchored or held up by the truth of certain metaphors that seem to me to enter poems when the time is right and the shape of the poem demands them. Used well, they allow the poet to transcend the merely biographical." If we look closely at what the poets in this book write about, O'Malley's description holds true as they explain the relationship between their lives and their poems. Byron's fasting, Ní Chuilleanáin's nuns, Newmann's Eve, O'Malley's seal woman, Boland's Anna Liffey, Strong's Mrs. Mahony, McGuckian's Crystal Night, and Ní Dhomhnaill's Grand-Aunt Elly are all metaphors that embody idea and feeling to move beyond ego and biography. However, recasting a legendary female figure or transforming a favorite aunt into an image often involves a process that these poets show is anchored strongly in the personal. As O'Malley says, the "poet is still, however pure, the author of what is recited." And if the "reciter" is a woman, the subject is often "woman."

Opening up the Irish poem beyond the limits of a traditionally male context introduces subjects, metaphors, and voices not often heard in the mainstream Irish poetic tradition. When Eavan Boland speaks in her essay of new "idioms," "vistas," and "perspectives," of women poets "enacting" a new form, and of new "expression" in the contemporary Irish poem, she is defining what many of the other essays in this volume illustrate. Nuala Ní Dhomhnaill argues persuasively that, for her, poetry represents the power to change the meaning of things. Returning at the end of her essay to the question posed at the beginning, "Who do you belong to?" Ní Dhomhnaill explains the value of poetry for her, even as she describes herself as displaced:

> I have had to make my home not in Ireland but in a version of Irish which is not just a language, but also a culture, a memory, and a fictional interaction with that memory. This is not without its plus sides—it gives me freedom to invent what I want *Irish* to mean, and in doing so to change it. Not knowing whom I belong to—being too Irish for embassy hangers-on and journalists, too English for Jacksaí Shea—is the price I pay for the power to change the meaning of things and for the freedom to make those changes available to others without distinction of nationality, through poetry.

While Ní Dhomhnaill is the only poet in this book who writes exclusively in Irish, the points she makes here are shared by many of the women writing in the following pages. What *Irish* can mean has been and continues to be a matter of debate, and, as I mentioned earlier, has included issues of politics, religion, language, and gender. Respect for the power to change fixed ideas about Ireland, Irish culture, Irish women, Irish poets, and the Irish poem is something these poets share; and what they have written suggests that envisioning such change often involves the creative transformation of experiences from their own lives into the metaphors and voices in their poems. Crossing boundaries—national, linguistic, cultural, geographic, religious, gender— gives the poet "freedom to make those changes available to others without distinction of nationality." In the voices we hear in this volume, Ní Dhomhnaill's statement "I don't belong to anyone. I belong to myself" echoes over and over again as these poets transform what Mary O'Malley calls "psychic cartography" into what *Irish* can mean and the Irish poem can be.

❧

Planning this volume, I asked each of the poets to consider the ideas associated with the words *woman*, *Irish*, and *poet* and to contribute both a prose piece and a poem that illustrated some of the points in that prose. The poems are placed before the prose to emphasize the links between them, to illustrate the relationship between autobiography and poetry, and to highlight the ways in which women poets manifest issues of identity and gender in their poems. In "Releasing Possibility into Form: Cultural Choice and the Woman Writer," Carol Watts sees gender reflected in literature not only in the "unconscious processes in artistic invention," but also in "a mastery of technical skills, and an often conscious manipulation of symbolic forms." It is "in their engagement with the demands of literary structures, which act as a locus of established meanings and an arena for alternative interpretive possibilities," Watts suggests, "that women writers have achieved a measure of self-realization" (1992:90). For the women in this volume, Irish poetry has become that arena of "interpretive possibilities"; they bring to it new perceptions and a vast array of female perspectives and experiences, images and voices. To return to my point at the beginning of this essay, the link between the poem and the poet's life can be both fascinating and enlightening. Poetry readings show us this all the time; so do the poems and prose that follow.

Eiléan Ní Chuilleanáin. Photograph by Macdara Woods.
Courtesy of Wake Forest University Press

Eiléan Ní Chuilleanáin

J'ai Mal á nos Dents

in memory of Anna Cullinane (Sister Mary Antony)

The Holy Father gave her leave
To return to her father's house
At seventy-eight years of age.

When young in the Franciscan house at Calais
She complained to the dentist, *I have a pain in our teeth—*
Her body dissolving out of her first mother
Her five sisters aching at home.

Her brother listened to news
Five times a morning on Radio Éireann
In Cork, as the Germans entered Calais.
Her name lay under the surface, he could not see her
Working all day with the sisters,
Stripping the hospital, loading the sick on lorries,
While Reverend Mother walked the wards and nourished them
With jugs of wine to hold their strength.
J'étais à moitié saoúle. It was done,
They lifted the old sisters on to the pig-cart
And the young walked out on the road to Desvres,
The wine still buzzing and the planes over their heads.

◁

Je mangerai les pissenlits par les racines.
A year before she died she lost her French accent
Going home in her habit to care for her sister Nora
(Une malade á soigner une malade).
They handed her back her body,
Its voices and its death.

(Ní Chuilleanáin 1989, 29)

Nuns: a Subject for a Woman Writer

Family

A photograph shows six women, six sisters, grouped in the garden of a suburban house in Cork in the 1940s. The parents are missing, so I know that it must have been taken after 1943, the year I was under one, the year of my grandparents' deaths. My father is missing too—was he the photographer? As their only brother, that seems the likely reason for his absence. The picture, however, came to me not from him but from the last of the sisters to die, in 1995, at the age of ninety-six. The event it commemorated was a rare one; at least two of them (depending on the year) would have been living abroad in the 1940s, and permission to go home was rarely given. I do not know if they were ever all together again in the family home.

Within the picture an important sub-group defines itself: the three who had entered religion—been reborn, changed their original names, left their families behind—between 1930 and 1936. (The Psalm had been sung over them: *Hearken, O daughter, and see, and incline thy ear: and forget thy people and thy father's house.* But they had not forgotten.) The three nuns, Sister Augustine Francis, Sister Francesca Clara, and Sister Marie Antony are on the left, one standing and two sitting. On the right their eldest, third eldest, and second youngest sisters are "the girls," Bridie, Madge, and Nora, one sitting and two standing. Two triangles, one dark, one light. The women living at home are all, and are all to remain, unmarried; they lived together until their deaths. They take up notably less space than their religious sisters; they look gauche and shrinking, while the black habits of the others flow imposingly into the space available, the knotted white girdlecords of the two Franciscans wriggling against the dark coarse stuff, the three faces defined by sharply starched white linen coifs over which the finer black cloth of the veil flutters a little.

Photography in Ireland was then in a great ecclesiastical age. Bishops were snapped at eucharistic congresses and ordinations, in all their gold and finery, while dark priestly figures pointed[1] every street scene, and nuns brought up the rear of crocodiles[2] of winning infants. In the books of black and white photographs from the twenties, thirties, and forties which are being published now, the extreme visibility of the church, as much as it is evidence of the clericalism of the new Irish state, is also an effect of the costume originally intended to be respectably unassuming—and the love-affair between celluloid and darkness. Nuns are there—as in Yeats's "Among School Children"—as props to the new order, standing respectfully to one side but identifiable.

My six aunts, born between 1898 and 1907, aged between twenty-four and fifteen when the Irish Free State was born, belonged to the first cohort of women entering an independent Ireland, and their lives form a commentary on one aspect of the new political and ecclesiastical world that came into existence then. Though their fierce nationalism meant that they would hardly have married ex-soldiers, they belonged, too, to the generation that was deprived of the chance of marriage by the slaughter of young men in the Great War. The fact that three of six went into convents is perhaps less surprising, appears less a break with the world they knew, when their lives—active, troubled, but also sheltered and companionable—are compared to the equally protected, religious, and ritualized lives of the other three who remained in what was called the world.

So it seemed to me as a child. My aunts' house lives in my mind as a feeling of calm and affection, a view of the enamel kitchen table and, beyond, of the small window lighting the scrubbed back kitchen, and the sound of an aunt chopping kindling wood in a tiny yard. There were long evening prayers; the place was strewn with books of devotion and fonts for holy water; and the extravagantly historical Crucifixions over the brass bedsteads upstairs, the barer portrait of Matt Talbot which hung over the dining table, the pieces of furniture always polished and in their traditional places, the fine china and the delicately embroidered tea cloths all belonged to a life with room for both

1. Punctuated
2. Pairs

austerity and luxury. All together they made my lay aunts' home more like a convent than any ordinary house; and, as two of my nun aunts at different times spent long periods in Ireland, I had a good opportunity to compare convents with each other and with other houses. My experience in this way parallels that of women who went on to enter the religious life themselves: many of them would have had family connections, beloved and influential aunts who had not at all forgotten their own people. And they would have attended convent schools and—especially in boarding schools—known much of the pattern of the nuns' lives.

For a small child, visiting a convent was fun. There was lemonade and cake, there was a croquet lawn—I discovered that nuns' big skirts gave them an advantage when it came to cheating—and there was the interest one aroused by being small and belonging to one of the community. There was the fascination of watching the nuns greeting each other affectionately but formally with a kiss, something I approved of but saw rarely in ordinary Irish families. My clearest memory of a really early moment is of the oddity of seeing a nun running, her black masculine shoes and long skirts and her solid ankles. Later I realized that away from the convent wing there was their work, with the old and shabby and institutionalized. We saw the old people in the chapel, praying loudly, intensely, eccentrically. The nuns sang sweetly and straight at the glittering, cool, flowery altar.

A few years after that I visited, still as a niece, other convents in northern France and Belgium. The buildings were older, the food more exciting, the old people smelt strongly of garlic, and there was, incredibly, wine with meals. The one memory that is particular to my aunts is of the day I heard the youngest one, the superior of her Belgian convent, quarreling eloquently with her chaplain, who wanted her to get rid of some employees and give their jobs to returned *Pieds-noirs* from Algeria. I was impressed by her anger and her command of the French language; looking back, it seems plain that he must have boasted, somewhere, that he could get her to do as he pleased. When I went with her to the order's motherhouse at Desvres, the atmosphere was quite different—hospitable too, but also warm and relaxed as a small group of Irish sisters reminisced together, again in voluble French. A warm, fresh, complicated world.

By then I was a schoolgirl. With my family background it had always been clear to me that my aunts would have liked me to enter religion, and that my parents, perhaps especially my father (who, after all, had barely escaped his family's tidal pull towards celibacy), would not. At my first school I had not been taught by nuns but by some formidable Republican ladies who knew little about education. I remember the relief when I was moved to the calm of the Ursulines' school, on the tallest hill in mountainous Cork city. But I had that need to resist their orderly charm and make my resistance explicit, just as a few years later I couldn't keep my mouth shut and told the headhunter from the Civil Service at the careers meeting that I wouldn't apply to join a system where I would be sacked if I got married.

I was resisting but also, consciously, admiring. I was raised, I suppose, like other girls, issued with pink lipstick and high heels, my hair cut and curled. Why did I feel this titivating was an interference with my person worse than cutting off a novice's long hair? Our skirts at sixteen years of age were crinolined and stiff, our bodies bunched and bundled by the corset industry, our faces tentatively powdered and painted and our eyelashes and brows darkened so we looked like Snow White. The beehive puff of hair on the top of the head came as a relief when the fashions changed away from the permanent wave, but it meant tangling your hair with a comb. My physical ideal of femininity remained, and remains, the clean, pale, ageless face of a nun, the body which unself-consciously clothed itself in full plain cloth and moved as intently as a fish in water.

In our school the nuns had a dark grey petticoat, and over that a long skirt which they wore tucked up purposefully when they were working and moving around. When they entered the chapel, they loosened the skirt and it flowed right to the ground, almost covering their feet and making them suddenly graceful. They would do the same, entering the parlor, when the bishop visited. That practiced gesture at the belt, the sudden rush of loose cloth, seemed to me not only beautiful, the first time I saw it, but eloquent of the change in them, from fussy demanding workers to ceremonious players in the house of prayer. Twenty years later I saw a Moroccan woman perform the gesture in reverse, tucking up her long glittering embroidered caftan into her belt so that her knee-length bloomers showed as she addressed herself—bending from the hips, with a floorcloth—to a floor where sugary mint tea had been spilt. The same freedom of the body, within its clothes.

⁀

I record all these things because they suggest so much to me still about women and their history. In my aunts' lifetimes there is another, better known, story of Irish women's lives, the story of their confinement to home and maternity, of their defeat or marginalization as workers, of Magdalens and typists, of mental patients, tuberculosis sufferers, of teachers and farmers. But there were also the women who lived in the enclosed world they had chosen, in communities of sisterhood. Their history is no odder, surely, than the history of armies, which have been close to the center of almost every state that has ever existed. Yet I cannot pretend not to notice, alongside the absolute ordinariness of that life in the traditional world, how strange it looks now to so many people—and did so then to some. Especially men. An uncle said to me, commenting on the subject of a few of my poems, "When I see a nun I always think, 'none.'" The feminine as lack and privation, most intensely seen in women who have neither man nor need for man.

Any poet needs to find a subject and a vantage point to view it from. When I began to write, I consciously used mythology, and natural and urban scenery. Unexpectedly I found then, in my late twenties, that the figure of a nun would be standing quietly in the middle of a poem, as in a room in my house, before I had asked her in. At other times she would be a hermit, or some other recollected female figure, darkly dressed and firm-faced. I even took occasional evasive action, deciding against the use of such imagery. But it kept suggesting itself, and each time it did I responded to that mixture of "strangeness and familiarity," as we call it. In my case what this phrase means is: something really strange, which I know that I, and before me many other women, have known with familiarity, even intimacy.

The preoccupation with nuns, and the reasons for their existence, explains or rather provides always the first syllable of an explanation of the world I grew up in and the many worlds I inherit. And to write poetry I need a theme that is really there, not made up, but intractably in the world I and others have lived in, hard and resistant to explanation, just like a word of which one possesses the first syllable, inexplicably having to keep reaching out for the rest. Since I am Irish—indeed, since I am human—the world I live in has to include the past as well as liberation from the past. Even though I know, for example, that nowadays nuns do not give up all outside correspondence for Lent, it comes back to me with a rush of understanding that as a schoolgirl I would have known better than to write a letter to my aunt before Easter. That single fact from the past carries meaning, about isolation, about sacred time, and about women's history, that makes it a possible subject—though I may never write the poem.

A woman writer must have a female voice. Does the voice come from the subject? I remember the day I put the word *arse* in a poem, and knowing that

I was deviating from a previously unconscious standard—I had not ever before used a word I hadn't heard in my mother's voice. But a body needs an arse and I needed the word because it was there. It seemed to me that it was not language or image but subject that really defined me as a poet; I wished to look at the feminine condition through the equal glass of the common language, making it my subject on my own terms. Was a female subject one which came merely from an assemblage of concerns that have been brushed into the corner labeled "women"? I had thought of writing about housework, service and so on, and found that I was making up an interest in such subjects which was totally unrelated to my life. Then I saw in memory a nun working, sewing, polishing, writing, looking after an altar and relics, loading patients on lorries in a war, speaking in a special nun's language, lying sick or dead in a room next to a laundry; and my sense of a living subject kindled at once.

The subject appeared to me in two guises, historical and physical. I was fascinated by the whole history of nuns in Ireland, as they appeared to exist on a border, both inside and outside Irish society. And my curiosity was drawn to the way their lives, their attention, were disciplined and directed to the physical world at all times, because it seemed a special case of the way women's lives have been lived.

History

The late nineteenth and the early twentieth centuries were the moment of the greatest flourishing of the conventual life not only in Ireland, but also, I think, worldwide among English-speaking people. Early Irish monastic foundations included many for women, headed by remarkable saints, aggressive creatures such as Gobnait, patron of beekeepers, who set her bees on robbers attacking her convent, or Brighid, who sent her nuns running to the four points of the compass with her miraculously expanding cloak because the king of Leinster had promised her as much land as her cloak would cover. She ended ruling over the plains of Kildare, a Dido with no false lover, no fatal pyre. Later houses of women belonged to the international orders: Benedictines, Cistercians, Dominicans, Poor Clares, Augustinians. They survived into Penal times, some of them refounded abroad like the Irish Benedictines of Ypres, repatriated at last in the Great War to Kylemore in County Galway. Others existed as covert communities in Ireland, as we can see by the occasional bequest to a "Mrs. ———, and the gentlewomen dwelling with her in her house."

With the relaxation and final abolition of most anti-Catholic laws, other or-
ders of nuns arrived from the Continent or were founded at home. They be-
came important in education and in the beginnings of social work, in a few
cases (for example, working with prostitutes in the port town of Derry) mak-
ing contact with the informal groups of mostly Protestant "ladies" who had
undertaken charitable works.

Some Continental nuns were at that point more snobbish than the natives,
and a class division was to persist. (They were not all ancient sisterhoods: the
nineteenth century saw many new orders founded in Europe too.) They pro-
vided what was much in demand, ladylike training for the daughters of the
Catholic middle class and remaining gentry. Women's education was more so-
cially stratified than men's, because a boy through education could leave his
origins behind if he was bright enough, whereas a girl's social standing was de-
termined entirely by her husband's, and the class of husband she would find
was in turn likely to depend on her father's status. Upper-class refinement
meant, in particular, the teaching of foreign languages and graces, and the
nuns trained in France and Belgium were well placed to supply them. Along
with the accomplishments they brought a culture of their own, expressed in
books and pious conventions of demeanor and gesture, and actively promoted
among their pupils. This too suited the society, which wished its young
women to partake of the monastic qualities of poverty, chastity, and obedience
so useful to their prospective husbands. Patrick Kavanagh's novels, for exam-
ple, describe the awkward reverence of the countryman for the convent-
educated girl as well as the savagery with which married women were treated.

I remember how, within the convent school, the ideals of worldly and reli-
gious etiquette, of genteel deportment were taught. Sanctity and self-denial
were propagated as part of the same education, and in fact that propaganda
was what offered an ideal of liberation. We were encouraged to be devout and
undertake minor penances; we were instructed on the correct posture for
prayer. We read the *Lives of the Saints,* and the majority of women saints were
nuns, especially foundresses. Their struggles were against themselves, against
worldly families or uncomprehending prelates; their achievements the setting
up of little groups of women prepared to give up all for the Lord. Their reward
was a lifetime of suffering contemplated on a glorious deathbed; there were
also wonderful episodes: visions, miracles, revelations, or just providential
pieces of good luck. We learned of the doubts of postulants, the harshness and
humiliation of novitiates, the problems of the leaders of communities. We

were half inside the convent ourselves, in what survived of a Catholic purdah, and we knew that the nuns were scanning each year's final class for potential recruits.

The books came from everywhere, the heroines were Catherine of Siena, Rose of Lima, Theresa of Avila, Thérèse of Lisieux—none or few were from English-speaking countries. The internationalism of the orders meant that many Irish women's experience, as pupils of the convent schools who in turn sent their daughters for the same teaching, must have responded to a groundswell of European as well as local history. It placed them, if they were alert, forever on the edges of their own society, which was itself until the 1920s a disaffected one, ill-disposed to the political center of the United Kingdom. The margin they occupied as women could sometimes be a vantage point, though it was connected with their political exclusion. It pointed away, to foreign places where dreams of the unknown potential of the woman's soul could be tested.

A STORY

A girl had packed her trunk to go off to a convent in Chicago. And in the last hour before going, she changed her mind. Her younger sister was down raking hay in the field, and she came in and said, "I'd love to go." And she went instead of her sister, and she was very happy.

Can the same vantage point, and the wonderful loosejointedness that is in that story, be of use to a woman writer? And need its usefulness be connected only with writing about women, their lives and culture? My mother, whose education all happened in a boarding school run by the Ursulines of Sligo, who never lost her affection for them or her sense of being in their debt, was a successful professional writer.[3] Although she wrote, as well as a number of "straight" novels, many books in "feminine" genres—children' s books, historical novels, detective stories—she made boys and men her central figures for the most part. She liked men and wanted to be read by them, and had observed that "girls will read a boys' story, but boys won't read a book written for girls." The girl is on the edge, looking in. And she made money by her

---

3. Ní Chuilleanáin's mother was the well-known writer Eilís Dillon.

writing, that final test of belonging to a "real" world. But she never wrote fiction about nuns.

The Irish classic on that subject is *The Land of Spices* by Kate O'Brien ([1941] 1988). Here a woman writer, whose own lesbian sexuality was an almost impossible theme for print in 1940, was successful in making the Irish Censorship Board look famously ridiculous. The book was banned for the phrase, "in the embrace of love" used about a glimpse of male homosexuality which is carefully placed and distanced in the past, in a foreign country, involving an Englishman and a Belgian boy. It is inserted in a longish chaste novel which is otherwise about boarding-school life, provincial Ireland, provincial Belgium, the childhood of a Reverend Mother and of the children in her school—and about Irish cultural politics and religious poetry, and spiritual and intellectual history in the international Catholic convent world between 1900 and 1914.

But just as the glimpse is what sends an eighteen-year-old into the novitiate, the phrase describing it does resonate powerfully; it is the clip that pins the book to all the books that might have been written on the subject of unpopular loves and obsessions such as that for the religious life itself. By 1940 the convent, especially as matrix of the convent school but also of the orphanage and the Magdalen home, was no longer marginal to Irish society. It was often an important focus of local life in small towns, and it was charged with the enforcement of much social consensus about the place and fate of certain women and children. O'Brien's theme, the sense of a feminine vocation, of a liberation from social constraints as wild as that of any girl who caused a scandal in her parish, was less likely to arouse general interest. It is her sureness of touch as she forces readers to see the connection that gives her novel its integrity.

A feminine tradition seems a difficult thing to establish in literature outside prose fiction. In poetry, women writing in Irish have at least a slender line to grasp at, through a succession looking to a fairly distant past, to Eibhlín Ní Chonaill, Máire Ní Laoghaire, and the fragmentary records of the keening women. They are at least no worse off than the men, reaching like them across a gap that yawns between fine modern writers, like Máire Mhac an tSaoi and Caitlín Maude, and the living tradition of women's poetry still alive in the early nineteenth century. Women writing in Irish now are helped by the scholarly and archaizing tendency of Gaelic culture as a whole, while an Irish woman writing in the international void of English has to define herself in relation to a vital masculine tradition and to reach out to a rapidly developing movement of women's writing all over the world. To look back to earlier Irish women writers in English seems difficult—though the republication of Katherine Tynan and others may be a sign that the recuperation of women's writing in Ireland has begun.[4]

In many countries women writers have seen themselves as giving a voice to a stifled feminine past and have tended to ignore the words in which that past speaks for itself. And then, our lives seem discontinuous with the culture of the past: our link with women of past centuries is almost reduced to the bodily fact as essential femininity. "Anatomy is destiny" is not a position that appeals to many feminists. Women's historians have concentrated instead on showing how women's physiology was invented and imposed on their bodies by a scientific establishment.

Nuns stand aside from this fragmented tradition. Their own succession is not bodily but adoptive and saturated with custom. A twentieth-century nun is closer to Hildegarde or Hrotsvitha than a twentieth-century bank teller can be to a Restoration maidservant, though all four may share literacy and the ethic of work. It is not merely the reiterations of prayer and the persistence of ideas that bind them but the totality and internationalism of a way of life. Studies like Patricia Curran' s *Grace Before Meals* (1989) or *The Crannied Wall* by Craig Monson (1992) illustrate both the persistence of rigid tradition into modern times and the openings that have so frequently existed, across the centuries, for creativity in the convent.

Body

I started from my fascination with the physical, with the body and the clothes. As a little girl I was taken aback by the complication of adults' clothes, the corsets and stiff hats and high heels. The nuns' clothes were plainer, but there was that starched wimple which made their heads like flowers. Over it the veil (emblem, it turned out, when I read the Ceremony of Clothing, of silence and

4. Eilís Ní Dhuibhne's *Voices on the Wind, Women Poets of the Celtic Twilight* (1995) includes the work of Tynan, Susan Mitchell, Dora Sigerson Shorter, Ethna Carbery, Eva Gore-Booth, and Nora Hopper Chesson.

submission), but which looked formidable, like a lion's mane or a cobra's hood, something to make the head bigger and more intimidating. And they wore shoes like my father's and were studded with lots of pins.

I stress these details because the life of nuns has always been entangled with the physical and concrete. Though they have counted writers, mystics, scientific researchers among them, they have been directed to practical work by the clerical bias against formally recognizing women's education or encouraging them to transcend the material world. Their formation too was based on the tradition of manual occupations for girls, even those of the highest social standing, and on strict surveillance which insisted they remain as it were *inside* their bodies, treating them as shelters to hide in, cultivating stillness and silence except for the fantastically active fingers.

More than ten years ago I visited a museum of Popular Arts in Malaga. Among the exhibits were many mass-produced, crude, brightly colored prints, posters, and picture-books; but alongside them was the almost impossibly fine needlework of convents, the eye-killing stitchery, white on white, devoted to altarcloths, veils for monstrances, envelopes for the keys to shrines. There were also less sacred products: ribbon weaving, beadwork, frail baskets of wheat straw, pictures made with the husks of grain or tiny shells. Between them they suggested what different things the desire to make and have artworks has meant: the impatience of the marketplace cheapjack, the appetite of religion for infinitely fine craft, and the endless unvalued world of women's secular time, contained and enclosed in work such as this. And the need felt by societies to keep women enclosed and occupied in inarticulate work. Even the fact that women's art came under the heading of "Popular."

I felt revulsion in the museum. I felt how much more valuable was the work of the Portuguese lay sister in Belgium whose work, of farmyard and kitchen, issued and was consumed in delicious food for the convent and its guests, whereas the products of secular leisure created in themselves problems which replicated the original problems of women's time: of attendance, grooming, use versus beauty. Yet by looking at such fragile and economically insignificant productions, we may be able to recuperate not merely the activities of past generations of women but the spirit of their lost culture. The fidgety crafts come from the leisure of women whose work was contemplation and prayer.

SAYINGS

One labourer to another who is attempting to rescue a nun from a hole in the road, into which she has fallen: "Don't touch her, Jem, she's consecrated. Use the shovel!"

—Cork joke

If you give the Poor Clares five pounds to pray for you, you'll always get an idea for a picture.

—A Dublin artist

Lord preserve us from the Sisters of Mercy.
—Attributed to the Plain People of Ireland

If your father hadn't persuaded me, I'd have gone into the convent.
—Attributed to the Mothers of Ireland

Scandal and the 1990s

As I write, the world of Irish women religious is disturbed by scandals from the past. Women from orphanages, Magdalen homes, mother-and-baby homes—and their families—are insisting on the stories of these places—their loneliness, hardship, and not infrequent cruelty—being told. The Irish appetite for history asserts itself again, demanding recognition for events which were supposed to be outside history. As so often in the past thirty or so years, it is clear that the politics of Catholic Ireland are centered on the personal, sexual, and familial and that the live issues of the day spring from the need to acknowledge the past. While nuns figure in the stories that are being told now, they are flanked by other, perhaps the real authority figures: priests, doctors, and policemen. In the background are the politicians and bureaucrats who decide how little would be paid, and when nothing would be paid, for the upkeep of the powerless.

These authority figures in turn were operating in a world of consensus, where concealment of family shame and the rigorous disciplining of children were unquestioned values. The protests about the regimes of Castlepollard,

Goldenbridge, and the Gloucester Street Laundry[5] are unlike the scandals of clerics sexually abusing children which preceded them in the news. Those stories aroused anger because the clerical caste seemed to be closing ranks to conceal behavior which, if known, would have been generally execrated. What is being blamed and rejected now is a whole social system, in which most children were regularly beaten by their parents as well as at school, and the children were told it was good for them, just as it was good for pregnant girls to be incarcerated.

My mother in 1961 had to bully a hospital into admitting an unmarried woman, eight months pregnant and with high blood-pressure. The hospital wanted, on the bishop's blanket instructions, to refer her to a home where treatment for her toxemia would not have been available, and her baby and perhaps she would have died.

A bus conductor looked with distaste at my sister and me on the way to school because he could tell by the uniform that we went to a place which did not allow pupils to be beaten. He told us with relish that we should be with the Mercy nuns at St. Aloysius's, where corporal punishment flourished. His resentment was also based on class: the Ursulines charged more.

Some time ago I heard a politician, about my age, recalling on the radio—in an almost casual way—how his mother "would cut a stick from the hedge and beat you till you couldn't stand," and how, once, when he tapped his daughter with his finger's ends, he was so horrified by her grief that he never did it again.

A great deal changed in Ireland in the 1960s and 70s, not simply attitudes to patriarchy and the church. The great decline of the Irish population was halted, the average age of marriage dropped sharply, and the great cohorts of the unmarried which had been a significant feature of Irish society—as indeed of most traditional societies—were greatly reduced. The legal and economic position of women improved as well as their physical health. Education became almost free, and corporal punishment was banned in classrooms. Tolerance spread gradually, and while the visible presence of unmarried mothers

5. Three institutions run by religious groups in Ireland, the source of recent scandals involving abusive treatment of women and children. Castlepollard was a mother-and-baby home, Goldenbridge an orphanage, and the Gloucester Street Laundry one of the Magdalen Laundries where unmarried pregnant women were hidden away and often forced to give up their babies for adoption.

was one visible sign of the change, another was the lessening of the embarrassment caused to women who left the religious orders, and to their families. Many did leave, but many stayed, and young women still did, and still do, choose that life. And many nuns are even more highly respected than before, less now for their sanctity and prayers than for their work in the community, of which they have become in some cases the uncomfortable conscience. Their history too has begun to be written, in some cases a painful one, but a story that is entwined with the emerging history of women in Ireland.

For someone who has always been interested in the subject, recent developments have meant realizing again how large and complicated the subject is. As a writer I am drawn to its long past of silence and turning away from the world, to my own memories of hospitality and humor, to the image it offers of a community of women interacting with formality and grace, to the seriousness and passion that was the source for all the sisters' work.

Mary O'Malley. Photograph by Joe Shaughnessey.

Mary O'Malley

Weakness

I come from a line of strong women
mostly dark, all carved from a harder rock
than me. I am the thin fault
that runs through the seam, a wave of quartz
surfing through granite, condemned to masquerade.
I am where history breaks and divides.
Brittle and weak, I have been cast down
before the upright women of my tribe,
ashamed before their silent eyes.

I carry weakness like a plague of tears.
They ignore it with the unassailable
mercy of their gaze that has not wavered once
in six thousand years and never lies—
only the strong survive. I am spared
for a doubtful task. They bear me up,
knowing I am only fit for dreams.
There I live mostly, avoiding funerals,
tracking the shapes that wheel across their heavens.

Nightly I enter the dark cave's mouth
where waves of whispering women
clamour to be heard. Surf brushes sand

in a softer language, the only tender thing
they had. The thread of my grandmother's voice
guides me through a labyrinth of syllables.
She knows my tendency to wander and get lost.
Daily I unravel voices from a choir of ghosts
and transcribe the blazing cyphers of my past.

(O'Malley 1993, 31)

"Between the Snow and the Huge Roses"

1

I grew up as a colonized child, linguistically speaking, but I had certain advantages. Long before I heard either the word "poem" or "theater," I had experienced the power of the mask. There is a tradition of unaccompanied singing in Ireland called *sean-nos,* meaning "old-style." The great *sean-nos* singer must become the impassive mask through which the song is sung. The style is handed down and, although each singer adds his or her own ornamentation, the form is clear and the song is all. The emotion engendered in the audience is often palpable, but the singer remains impassive, a perfect mask. Such singing is a high art form and the opposite of the often maudlin sentimental songs so popular among immigrants and in pubs, which served their own, quite different purpose. The great *sean-nos* singer becomes what Yeats would have us believe the true poet must achieve. Such possession by the muse is rarely as achievable in poetry as in song or theater, since the poet is still, however pure, the author of what is recited. Still when I read Heaney's clear explanation of Yeats's belief in the poet as mask (1988, 148), allowing the archetypal voice to possess him, I recognized a true note. That is not, of course, the whole story.

Let me be clear from the start—I agree with Heaney that the poet needs to go beyond ego to become more than the voice of autobiography (1988, 149). I agree equally with Eavan Boland that poetry enters where myth touches history (1995, 166). Since history and story were very close relations for me, I take that to include personal history. Since I grew up with a very real and local mythos that arose out of the ritual activities of the place I lived in, myth was the more powerful and less subjective of the two. I am a fisherman's daughter and a blacksmith's niece and was surrounded by strong shapes and deep rhythms from the time I could talk. It is these shapes and their essential strength that I intend to explore here. Put simply, I am anchored or held up by the truth of certain metaphors that seem to me to enter poems when the time is right and the shape of the poem demands them. Used well, they allow the poet to transcend the merely biographical.

2

I was born on the west coast of Ireland in the 1950s. People were poor in those days, and deaths, births and weddings provided what later became known as a social life. That phrase came into vogue in Connemara in the seventies and was always uttered as you would a foreign phrase or some youthful slang—a little mockingly, or tentatively and with more than a hint of sarcasm. As in "The next thing the women will be looking for is a 'social life.' " I lived in a world of limited vocabulary and rich conversation. The language I learned was layered and resonant, but we were often unsure of those words or phrases that came in from books and the radio. People enjoyed experimenting with them, but new or big words needed a decent interval before they were accepted. Also, you risked social ridicule by showing off too many or using them too soon.

Anyhow, the main events were centered around the church, and outside of the three already named, Mass, confession, and Holy Days provided the rest of the fun. Best of those was St. Cailin's Day, when cousins and friends from the Irish-speaking parts of Connemara arrived and, after doing the pilgrimage to the well, all would go back to my grandmother's house for refreshment. The pilgrimage consisted of circumambulating the holy well seven times and saying a decade of the rosary on each round. A stone was dropped in at the completion of each circle. The sea was cold and grey against the rocks below.

I was allowed out in the currach, and later the bigger boats, with my father. Those boats were lovely but far from romantic. I learned that early, my stomach heaving as the boat slapped around in the swell while lobster pots were hauled or set. In winter I used to go to the forge and wait for permission to reach up and grab the handle of the huge bellows, then swing down with all my might and up again as the great lung filled with air. As I bore down, the air would rush out and the fire would blaze until it was red-hot and ready for the iron. Years later the forge came to mind as I read Adrienne Rich's comments on certain material being so hot that the writer needed asbestos gloves with which to handle it (1979). The gloves were, of course, a strong shape or form.

I am aware that such recognition only takes me so far intellectually, but it takes me much farther poetically.

3

The shapes of my childhood were clear and sustained me in a way that access to an early literary education and debate might otherwise have done. I am not saying that my experience was a poor substitute—only that it was what I had, and it was enough. Horseshoes, altars, anvils. Hooks and gaffs, nets and lobster pots which I helped make. Intricate stitches in Aran jumpers. There was little room for mistakes, and naming things was important. I knew the need for craft and skill early, and I knew that in the right combination of the two could lie the difference between life and death. Then, occasionally there was beauty, a shape or object that had use but was also lovely—the lure on a fishing line, the lead weights my father made, the wrought iron gates and candlesticks my uncle fashioned. Objects, however beautiful, only lasted if they were well made. Vessels of great beauty had to be sound in a storm. I could wish there had been more frivolity, more decoration, but there wasn't for anyone in rural Ireland then. Years later I apply those standards instinctively learned to a sonnet or a quatrain and especially to the rare elusive villanelle. Will it hold up the poem and float it, or is it the wrong vessel for the job in hand? And, just as relevant, can I fashion it well enough?

Needless to say, all this went on unconsciously, and I avoided bringing the raw material of my past into poems for many years, until eventually it imposed itself with such vehemence that it could no longer be ignored. There is a powerful passage in Eavan Boland's *Object Lessons* (1995, 166–74), where a neat suburban scene darkens and the detail, as she writes, hardens. The presence of an ancestor is superimposed on the street. The past becomes unavoidable if truth is to be served. I never had the luxury of distance from that past. At my most resistant, I knew it was only a matter of time, of honing skills. The ancestors were always there, and they insisted on their due, my second collection. The famine was as real to me from my grandmother's stories as Ireland joining the Common Market. Politics was the civil war and the gaping dike of the border, and Derry in flames was superimposed on images of the GPO in 1916. A man landed on the moon. I stayed up nearly all night with my father to marvel at it. It was like a miracle. In such a way did the centuries collide in our house.

Hardly historical accuracy, but then what is? There were few women in history and no babies and none of the stories from the famine. It was mentioned, written about in a way that only people who didn't believe in it would write. We had our own way of holding out against a version of history that left us out, either because we were politically awkward or quite simply did not matter. We had myth and song to preserve our stories, our belief in ourselves.

4

Structure and sensuality were provided in the theater of the church, with its incense and mystery and sacraments, the lovely copies of Italian religious paintings depicting the fourteen stations of Christ's agony and the gold shining like the lost innocence of angels. Then there was ritual and all in Latin, the calls and responses that echoed across a darkened church at the Easter ceremonies. Above all, the feeling of being absolved. I wanted to be a saint, but not, however, by way of the convent. Nuns, we frequently told one another in fits of giggles, would die wondering. The church, in a way, also provided sin—original, mortal, venial, and all to do with sex. We were warned about the perils of going to work in England and losing your religion. This was especially dangerous for women and only led to the one thing.

So did staying at home, alas, and in those days that did not include becoming a writer. Not because of your sex, but because of your background. Fishermen's daughters didn't become teachers either, but it was a better bet than my other ambition, which was to become the first woman skipper in Ireland. My father never discouraged me even in that, but I think he knew I wasn't tough enough. As it happened, I decided to go at it slant, as they say, and aim to become a teacher.

I was raised between languages. This matters, increasingly. The deep structure and much of the syntax of the language I spoke was Irish. I lived in a place suited to that language and the sensibilities of its people. We spoke English, but almost the entire specialized vocabulary of the sea, the names of fish, rocks, birds, and plants was in Irish. To this day I am occasionally unsure of whether certain words are in Irish or English. And I loved Irish and found it easy to read and write. There were words that resonated only in that language. Many of them were words I didn't have, but when I heard or even read them they fell neatly, perfectly, into a space already prepared and I knew their meaning instantly. This happened when poetry came to me and I to it, first when I was able to read and recite, then increasingly, in secondary school. It was wonderful that here was one task dreaded by most of my schoolmates which I loved. The reason was of course simple. The rhythms and sounds, what Frost called "the sound of sense," were most immediate in the language I had lost. But I had no confidence in speaking it because I knew I spoke it badly. And I had had enough of feeling inadequate in English, in front of summer visitors whose accents and linguistic ease seemed to give them a sense of entitlement. As a child, I knew I was as entitled as anyone else; I never felt stupid, but I knew that I often made mistakes in grammar and pronunciation, and it mattered terribly because I needed to be fluent and articulate.

5

Perhaps because I had nothing else. Yet it was not that simple. If there was often an arrogance that went with being highly articulate, there was also an ease and grace that spoke of a privileged world of books and music to which I needed to gain entry. However, I always believed that I had an absolute right to that world, the world of the Big House, that it had been built on the backs of my people, as it were. What caused me real pain was being inarticulate in the language that was mine by right, whose rhythms ran under the English I spoke every day, which was my grandmother's first language and which I would not ruin by speaking badly.

I will always remember the morning I went to my first Irish lecture in university. The level of spoken Irish was too high for me, or as I saw it, my standard was too low, and I left the lecture ashamed. As some kind of penance I changed to economics, in which I had absolutely no interest and which I endured for a year. I now realize that the penance was as much the lecturer's as mine.

It was as well, then, that I had true metaphors that would see me through the tangle of consonants and nouns and diphthongs that ran through my head like Séan Ó'Riordáin's pack of untamable thoughts, anarchic and dangerous. Especially since I was reading and being seduced by Coleridge and Donne at the same time as Seathrun Ceitinn and Máire Mhac an tSaoi were challenging me in Irish.

What I felt in those years, all the rage and shame and anger, was not unique. When I read John Montague's magnificent book *The Rough Field* (1989), I felt as though here was someone who felt as I did, but knew it to be the legacy of history:

A Severed Head

The master
gouges another mark
on the tally stick
hung about its neck

Like a bell
on a cow, a hobble
on a straying goat.
To slur and stumble

in shame
the altered syllables
of your own name; . . .

. . . .

Decades later
that child's grandchild's
speech stumbles over lost
syllables of an old order.

6

It has never been as well expressed in English. That book released and inspired me, and it inspires me still. The right lines can cut through darkness like a comet. After reading *The Rough Field*, I gave myself permission, as it were, to write of the place where I was raised. The result, a collection entitled *Where the Rocks Float* (1993), is dedicated to my grandmother. She was one of the gentlest women I have ever met, and one of the bravest, and she had a lovely voice. She has been my guide in troubled times since well before her death. She lived to see television enter a house previously dominated by the radio and conversation, and she loved it. She could now entertain the Pope; and once John F. Kennedy appeared, footage from before he was shot. She loved Kojak and shouted out to warn him of any danger. She could be caustic too at times: "You better hurry up and catch them, you've only ten minutes left," she'd say if the detective wasn't up to his usual standard. Television enriched her life by providing her with extra visitors but, never a passive viewer, she dominated it. She filled my life with stories—of the famine, the castle, the Black and Tans. Her journey to America when she was only sixteen was my first epic. As indeed it ought to have been. She was, like my father, an avid reader and made me read aloud to her when her sight was failing. She'd tell me poems and rhymes and more stories. Her patchwork quilt is a poem now, and hers is the hand holding the thread that guides me through the labyrinth in the poem "Weakness" (O'Malley, 1993, 31).

⌐

I need strong shapes to write about the sea. Richard Murphy, a poet to whom I owe a great deal and whose book, *Sailing to an Island* (1963), I carried around with me like a talisman for all the years I lived in Portugal, said somewhere that he wanted to write about the sea, so he bought a boat and learned to sail her. The other book I carried during those years was by Federico García Lorca. I was away from Ireland and glad to be gone. I loved Lisbon—the freedom of a country just a few years after a Revolution—where, to quote Lorca, "the night became as intimate as a little square" (1960, 39). I felt at home in my body, and in a way that would never be allowed in Ireland. It was as if the other half of me had come alive.

Those were radiant years, the other side of sin. And I discovered the poetry of Fernando Pessoa and his three other personae[1] and poured hot chocolate from ornate silver pots in the Edwardian cafe he had frequented in the Praca de Figuera. I heard fado and samba and deeper, more joyous rhythms from Brazil and Mozambique. I fell in love with a European capital for the first time. Lisbon is a watery city with a marine light. Every morning I passed the spot Columbus is reputed to have set out from on his journey to the other world.

7

Pablo Neruda's voice became insistent here:

Barcarole

Como ausencia extendida, como campana subita,
El mar reparte el sonido del corazon,

---

1. Alvaro de Campos, Alberto Caiero, Ricardo Reis were three pen names Pessoa used.

[Like absence spun out, like a sudden bell,
the sea shares out the heart's own sound.]

And above all:

La Poesía

Yo no sabía qué decir, mi boca
no sabía
nombrar,
mis ojos eran ciegos,
y algo golpeaba en mi alma,
fiebre o alas perdidas,
y me fui haciendo solo,
descifrando
aquella quemadura,
y escribi la primera línea vaga.

[Poetry

I did not know what to say, my mouth
had no way
with names,
my eyes were blind,
and something started in my soul,
fever or forgotten wings,
and I made my own way,
deciphering
that fire, and I wrote the first faint line.]
                    (1970, 457)

I return to him now to give me courage and faith, as I turn to Ted Hughes for
toughness and to Eavan Boland for that intellectual clarity that I admire.

From *The Double Vision of Manannan* (eighth century):

The clear ocean seems
A marvel of beauty to Bran

In his currach; but mine
Rides a flowering plain.

Those bright waves
Under the prow of Bran
To my double-rimmed chariot
Are blossoms of the Honey Plain.[2]

8

The sea was always there. The other half of the double vision. Treacherous and likely to betray. The only place I feel complete and am not afraid. Neruda knew it and knew what it could do. He was not afraid of the passion in this most seductive of elements and the most dangerous to the poet. Not quite respectable, somehow. Not like fire. A bit . . . murky. Conrad, a man's man, had captured its power and grit, but what about Walcott? There are men I'd rather have steering me through a force ten gale but I applaud the risk in both poets' work. Theirs, of course, were warmer oceans.

II

Now let me start again and tell the truth another way. Without the filter. I was raised at the edge of the sea in hard times in a place where you had to be tough to survive. The women were strong and able for death and birth and disappointment and the men . . . who knows? They rarely confided, in words. There was singing and dancing and silence like a high wall surrounding certain areas of life, and the greatest sins were weakness and making a fuss. I was guilty of both. Worse, I loved poetry and dreamed of a different life. Not even a specific kind of life, just . . . more.

I didn't fit easily into the circle of convent girls and women. A place in such a group has to be earned, and though I wanted to get in, badly at times, I never quite knew how. Perhaps being apart is a necessary part of the artist's

2. Translation by John Montague in *The Faber Book of Irish Verse* (1974, 45–47). When the Irish mythological hero Bran traveled over water to visit Emhain, the magical island of women, he met Manannan, whose chariot was crossing the waves as if it were on land. After a year on the island, Bran, against the warnings of his lover, tried to return to Ireland but eventually perished. The story is one of many in which water is seen as the source of both happiness and destruction.

training. Life can be made very uncomfortable when you are kept out. This is how the seal woman might feel.[3] Yet she has a life of great richness and she sees things with a rare intensity. The truth is that she wants friends but lacks the commitment they seem to require. Her interests are different from theirs. Suspiciously different. She is not, quite, in her own element.

The village was lovely, and when I first left it to go to university, I couldn't sleep for weeks because I missed the sound of the waves. The contours of the land and shore had left their marks on me, a kind of psychic cartography whose lines were drawn, ready for the day I would have need of them.

9

I learned the value of form and discipline, but I was raised to be anarchic. There was a wildness that survived, an edge, though I was an obedient child, afraid of breaking rules. I had a deep suspicion of the government. The first time I ever saw a guard I ran crying to my mother, thinking he was going to kill us all. I got him confused with the bogeyman. This might have been because some people often called the guards "peelers," a pejorative term referring back to the days before independence.[4] I believed in God and magic and the brittle old rose my aunt kept wrapped in tissue paper. She had found it on the pillow of her youngest daughter, a sign from heaven, whence it had fallen. I looked at the brown petals in wonder, in a house miles from anywhere except the Slyne Head lighthouse, with the sand blown up over the deep sill of the kitchen window. I used to sit there on the hob, watching my aunt put bread soda and salt into the little niches beside the fire. Inside, all was domestic and cushioned; outside, the elements tore at the house and threatened to engulf it. When I read Isabel Allende, I wondered why the house of the spirits was so familiar to me. I think I was prepared for it well before I could read.

In some sense that is what a house is—a space carved in a maelstrom of

---

3. The seal woman, who appears in the mythiology of several coastal areas, including Ireland, is a sea figure who occasionally visits land and mixes with humans but is always drawn back to the sea.

4. The word "peeler" is derived from Sir Robert Peel, prime minister of Great Britain (1834–35, 1841–46), who as secretary for Ireland was responsible for developing the British forces who policed Ireland.

chaos, a stone citadel that will keep our children from the abyss and show hospitality to friends and strangers. Small wonder that a critic once remarked that there was little domestic detail in my poems. Yet the house on the headland was comfortable and, like my bedroom at home, lit at night by the double arc of the lighthouse. A place to indulge yourself. Maybe the pagan came through in such a wild place. The magic certainly did, laced with miracles and prayers.

Yet if I had never read Marques or Lorca, that strange world, full of mystery and possibility, might have faded, leaving only a nameless dissatisfaction.

In the Mercy convent where I went to secondary school, the Blessed Virgin was deafened with pleas from all sides. There was a notion that you'd be as well to bypass God and go straight to where the power was, the mother. She'd intercede for you. She was particularly busy in May and June, on account of the exams. The nuns knew how to get things done. These women had no need of men and paid little heed to them, though they were well aware of their capacity for doing damage. They were subservient to the priest, and a sort of comedy of manners was played out every time he visited. I grew uncomfortable with the women always leading from behind and, after reading the promise-of-publication letters written in his magazine,[5] found that St. Martin de Porres (from Peru, if I'm not mistaken) was the man for me.

10

St. Martin de Porres was called on for all kinds of favors, and I grew up fully believing that at any moment I could witness a miracle. I still do. Maybe I'll come home one day and find a neatly made dark man standing politely in my kitchen, nodding his head, dropping in to say hello in archaic Spanish. Or an Indian language I have never heard of. Or both. "You must be St. Martin," I'd say. "No hablo Ingles," he'd say politely. Maybe we had more in common than I realized.

The possibility of a visit from the marvelous is part of being a poet, but also intrinsically bound up with where I believe poetry comes from. From the other world, where else? Through those shapes and metaphors. I remember clearly my first encounter with Blake, the sinewy tiger burning in the dark. Then Hopkins drawing on complexity, putting it all in. No mannered under-

---

5. A promise to publicize, in a newspaper or magazine, a favor granted by the saint.

statement there. And MacNeice's timeless line from "Snow": "There is more than glass between the snow and the huge roses" (1949, 30).

There is a gap, a sort of geological fault, where myth touches history. There is a tectonic shift between languages where the plates of the old rub uneasily against the new. Out of such spaces I write. That is neither good nor bad; it is simply what informs me, and the wonder is that I never know between one poem and another what ghosts or visions the next tremor will release.

Nuala Ní Dhomhnaill. Photograph by Bernd Weisbrod.

Nuala Ní Dhomhnaill

In Memoriam Elly Ní Dhomhnaill (1884-1963)

She got an honours degree
in biology in Nineteen-four,
then went back to her homeland
at the butt of the hill,
its backside to the wind,
and stopped there all her days.
She never married.
No one around was good enough for her.
When her brother married,
his bride wasn't good enough for him,
in Elly's view, and
she sold their land.

She fought with her father.
She fought with her brother.
She fought with the P.P.
To her it was all wrong
that dues were read out aloud
in the middle of Mass.
She saw right well the cheek—
imposing on the poor
to pay the Church beyond their means
and leave their children hungry.

On that account, she'd sit
satisfied in her own pew,
hand on her blackthorn,
hat on her head,
awaiting the call from the altar,
"Elly O'Donnell—nothing."

The only one to visit her
was my father
—the family's pious Aeneas—
and when she went
she left him the house,
which we sold—too damp.
I promised to write to her
but didn't.
Maybe everything I've written since
has addressed itself to that proud spirit,
who had no call to lie
with a man her match.

My own man was warned off
when he met me
for fear of the same bad drop,
saying I was just like her,
a loner,
her sole heir.

In olden times
there was venom in the withering wind from Binn ós Gaoith
as our people were herded like cattle into Macha na Bó.
  (Ní Dhomhnaill 1990, 25–27; translation by George O'Brien)

Cé Leis Tú?

One late summer day when I was five, I was walking up the village of Cahira-trant, in Ventry parish, where I had been recently fostered out to my Aunt May to learn Irish.[1] Wrenched unceremoniously from my middle-class existence in Lancashire, I was coping rather dubiously with cows, dust roads, no running water or electricity, Irish, and the fact that nobody could understand my Scouse English, anymore than I could understand their Kerry accents. I met an old man, Jacsaí Shea, coming down the road towards me. "Cé leis tú?" he asked me [Who do you belong to?], which was the usual local way of asking a child their name. Taking the phrase at its most literal meaning, I drew myself bristling to my great height of all three foot nothing and stoutly replied, "Ní le héinne mé. Is liom féin mé féin" [I don't belong to anyone. I belong only to myself]. Chuckling mightily, Jacsaí continued down the road to the house of Peats Mhic Ó Cinnéide, which was the village Dáil, or Parliament, where the older men were wont to gather in the evening to discuss the affairs of the world, great and small. My encounter with Jacsaí was obviously part of the evening's entertain-ment, because the story went around the village like wildfire, and even now, forty years later, it is occasionally thrown in my face, especially when I have done or said something that is considered in the village to be a bit "bold" or "too in-dependent."

Such sauciness is inevitably put down to *dúchas,* or genetic heritage from "the other side," my father's bloodlines to the north of the peninsula, beyond the Connor Pass, *i dtaobh thíos de chnoc,* (below the hill), especially to my Grand-Aunt Elly that I am temperamentally supposed to be the dead spit of. I knew Elly slightly as a child, and was rather fond of her. Or, rather, she seemed to take a special interest in me, and liked what others considered my "cheeky" ways. I have always felt she was a woman before her time, independent and strong-willed, who had merely been given a very bad press, and have sought to correct the story somewhat by writing a poem about her. Elly was no angel, and I try to explain some of her more cantankerous behavior as the natural conse-quences of the hundreds of years of ill-treatment of the local people, who were used worse than wild animals from the time of the Elizabethans onwards.

1. A longer version of this essay appeared in the winter 2000 issue of *Eire-Ireland.*

But my youthful encounter with old Jacsaí is still the crux of the matter. Based on a semantic misunderstanding, it sums up inescapably my relationship with West Kerry; *of* the Gaeltacht, I am not *from* the Gaeltacht. The Diaspora has seen to that. Inexorably drawn to the Irish-speaking communities of the western seaboard, and knowing them intimately, I am still always an outsider, the little *cailín Sasanach,* or English girl, that I was then. It has cultivated what Seamus Heaney calls "a doubleness of focus, a capacity to live in two places at the one time and in two times at the one place, a capacity to acknowledge the claims of contradictory truths without having to choose between them." A capacity to be genuinely bilingual, to be at home in two languages, in very different mind-sets. I wonder about this a lot. Is it always, or necessarily, a good thing? Does it really, as many claim, lead to a genuinely stereoscopic and enriched view of life, or is it the cause of mental astigmatism and blurred vision, a sense of displacement, a deep anxiety? I have found at times that the inner contradictions it entails cause deep psychic pain. Sometimes it is as if a civil war were going on deep inside me, and the sheer effort of keeping a standoff of the warring parties is deeply exhausting. All my energies get sucked down into the subconscious, with depression, characterized by deep lethargy, as its most obvious physical manifestation. Even in better times there is a constant restlessness. Is this feeling of being unsettled, vaguely in exile from somewhere we know not where, or something we know not what, connected with the sheer complexity of Irish history, or is it rather just an ineradicable part of the modern condition? There is no Ithaca to return to; the cancerous spread of a global "pop" monoculture has seen to that.

⏽

If Jacsaí had asked me the more usual "Cad is ainm duit?" [What is your name?], there would have been no initial misunderstanding. Ask a simple question and you will get a simple answer. But Jacsaí was of an older generation, with a completely different *Weltanschauung,* which could no more imagine an unattached human being than he could identify a star without its surrounding constellations. The modern concept of an "individual" with unalienable "rights" had not yet percolated up out of the great seething and teeming collective amoeba which was the local Irish-speaking community. His was a genealogical imagination; it could go back at least seven generations on all sides, with all the entailing combinations and permutations, in what was in material terms a community of very small farmers, in a subsistence economy so poor that many might ask, "Why bother?"—all these people lived and married and had so many children and died, but none of them was *rich* or important. But that would be to entirely misunderstand the case. The people of Cahiratrant in the fifties may have been poor in a material sense, but linguistically and spiritually they were heirs not only to a collective oral culture going back millennia but also, because of the vagaries of history, to the literary and manuscript culture of medieval Irish as well. A line from a Fenian lay or an Old Irish saga was as apt to trip off their tongues as a remark about the difficulty of scuffling mangolds. As George Thomson put it in *Island Home: The Blasket Heritage:* "Every educated Greek is familiar with Homeric tales of the Trojan War, but only from literary sources; for after the introduction of Christianity the pagan stories were forgotten by the common people. In Ireland, too, many were lost in this way, but others have survived in oral tradition down to our time" (1988, 26).

⤳

What was true of the Blasket Islands was equally true of the parish of Ventry, from which many of the islanders had come originally. To this day many of the last of the ex-islanders are still buried in St. Catherine's Graveyard in Ventry, for this is their *fód dúchais,* or ancestral sod, though they have lived in Dunquin since their evacuation to the mainland in the early fifties. The generation who were adults in Cahiratrant when I was a small child were no different from their island relatives. Jacsaí, and Joeín Shea (no relation), Mike Long, Joe Keevane, Moss and Paddy Martin, John Shea, whose mother was my great-grandaunt, or Thomas Murphy, married to my Aunt May, they and many others like them were willy-nilly tradition bearers. For them, and therefore for us children listening to them, the whole landscape around was steeped in legendary memories of the past. One of the best loved of the Fenian tales, "The Battle of Ventry," had taken place on the very strand which met our eyes every day. This battle, which lasted for the mythical year and a day, had pitched the Fianna, as guardians of Ireland, against the forces of Dáire Donn, the King of the Eastern World. A medieval manuscript tale written by a monk in Regensberg, circa 1200 A.D., it was totally assimilated locally. Wasn't Dáire Donn's grave in the field behind the local national school, Scoil Chaitlíona, at Cill Mhic an Domhnaigh, and the big rock called Lic Caoil off Thomas Murphy's land at Barr na hAille, wasn't that the petrified body of the giant Caol mac Criomhthain, the last of the Fianna to be brought down? Didn't his body come in on the strand called after him to this day Tráigh Chaoil, when he was drowned while preventing the last surviving invader, Fiannachtach Fiaclach, from escaping? That large standing stone or *gallán* in Sheehy's field that we passed every day, wasn't that where the great queen, his wife, was buried when she dropped dead on the spot, after pouring out her grief in the great lament for her husband, *"Géisid cuan"*?

❧

One day, sitting in his favorite spot at the south-facing corner in the middle of the village, Mike Long told me how as a boy he had seen the main fleet of the British navy on maneuvers before the First World War sail into safe anchor in Ventry Bay. He and the other young lads of the village had rowed out to meet them and had been aboard many of the great vessels, including the flagships the HMS *Dartmouth* and the HMS *Falmouth* (on which my Cork granduncle was subsequently drowned when it went down with all hands in the Battle of Jutland). As Mike recounted it, "the masts of the ships were so thick in the bay you'd swear they were trees of the forest," and they "walked from the farthest out boat in onto the strand, going from deck to deck, without as much as wetting their feet once." I recognized both phrases as straight out of the medieval text of *The Battle of Ventry,* and my heart gave a little leap of joy. The First World War, the mythical Battle of Ventry, what difference?—they were all grist to the great mill of local and popular imagination. They fueled a conversational art of enormous elasticity, and wide-ranging mythological reference, and of a stylistic and syntactical elegance that was breathtaking. Or, as the Americans say, "to die for."

❧

And in that very last sentence lies a point crucial to my considerations. In Ireland everything, including personal and collective history, gets subsumed into the mythological. Our unconscious is still by far our most creative side. For one reason or another on this island, the door between the rational and the irrational has never been locked tight shut. There was always someone: the bard in the hall, the *seanchaí* by the fireside, or the balladeer in the pub who kept his foot in the door. Walter Ong describes this as a high level of residual orality (1971), and the spoken word, by its very nature and spontaneity, has a plumb line into the subconscious that, except for the very best fiction and poetry, literary activity very rarely has. I love this aspect of our culture. It is one of the main things that drew me back to live here, after years on the shaughraun.[2] It is infinitely more exciting and much more of a human challenge to

2. Wandering.

live in a country which is just intermittently in touch with the irrational than in one which has set its face resolutely against it. It is one of the reasons, I think, that the arts are in such a wonderfully creative state in Ireland at the moment. Art necessitates a holistic approach to life, at the very least the strong neck which is the necessary bridge between the head and the rest of the body, and no artistic creation which has been approached in a purely rational or logical manner is going to satisfy us aesthetically. Nevertheless, this great gift of ours is not without its drawbacks and its own inherent dangers, one of which is that, like children, we are so overwhelmed by our inner scenarios that we act them out in a public manner, without any awareness of the Reality Principle, or of the fact of other people's necessarily different reality. Collective hysteria is an example of this, and God knows, what with Moving Statues and whatnot, this country has had more than enough of the likes recently. Another problem with the telescoping of history and myth is that it can lead to an idealistic culture of sacrifice, which has been a part of Ireland's tragedies in this century. Poetry, which expresses these inner unconscious dynamisms and cosmographies, has often been blamed for fanning the fires of inner pathologies, rather than relieving them, and since the time of Plato at least has been given bad press on this account. I contend that this is a misreading of poetry, and that good poetry actually resolves these inner tensions, or at the very least holds them in abeyance. That these conflicting inner drives, when held together under enormous tension in the vessel of the psyche rather than being acted out blindly, are the stuff of poetry, which is the metamorphosed and greatly altered result of these tensions, issuing from the depths of the psyche under great pressure, like common carbon turns to diamonds in the fiery depths of the earth.

⁓

The worldview of the oral tradition is ahistoric, or rather telescopes the events of history into mythological time. This was brought home to me most strikingly on one particular occasion in my early teens. I had noticed from the perusal of some map or other that the townland of Cahiratrant was completely surrounded by another townland called Na Ráithíneacha, or "Rawheens" in English, where it seems to mean "Little Raths." I had never seen a townland so cut off before and so I questioned my aunt's husband, Thomas Murphy, about how this might have come about. In his typical mode of mock exasperation, he shot back at me, *"Ná fuil a fhios ag an saol go raibh an Treanntach ró-mhaith d'Fhionn Mac Cumhaill?"* [Doesn't the whole world know that de

Terraunt was too strong for Fionn Mac Cumhaill?]. This was the first inkling that I had ever had that "Rawheens" could be as easily, and probably more properly, construed as the plural of *Ráth Fhinn,* or "the Rath of Fionn." And so the whole historical drama of the Norman invasion and the erection of a manse by the conquering knight de Terraunt, thereby displacing the former Gaelic order, still shows up most succinctly in the townland names on a map and can by summed up by a local farmer in one sentence: *"Ná fuil a fhios ag an saol go raibh an Treanntach ró-mhaith d'Fhionn Mac Cumhaill."* For me as a poet, this wonderful heterogeneity of material is an advantage rather than a disadvantage, speaking as it does of a spontaneous eruption of unconscious material, with very little input from the organizing, linear left brain. It is an associative mode of thought which lends itself very easily to poetry. Thus many poems of mine grow naturally from the stories that I had heard in Cahiratrant as a child:

The Narrow Path (An Bóithrín Caol)

Behind my mother's house
down Bóithrín Caol,
over from Bóthar na Carraige,
through the land of the Kavanaghs
the people of Fán would journey
three miles to the strand
with horses bearing panniers
for sand to dress

their kitchen floors and byres;
sand trodden into dung
and then laid out at last
on thin potato fields
to grow prodigious *Champions*
conjured out of famished land
too lean to bed such promise.

With creels lashed
to their backs
women

used to clamber
down these cliffs
for sustenance of mussels.
Four young girls were lost
at Leacacha an Ré—
Three Marys and fair Margaret
who set my heart astray—
and people saw
a red-capped man
astride the wave
that took them under.

Sometimes from the strand
I seem to glimpse
that red cap
lustrous in the spume
flayed off the waves,
and then,
without a word
a piper from a rock
beneath the cliff
releases drone
and chanter.
When horses
turn at nightfall,
swaying under sand,
the men who lead them home
chatter no longer.

(Ní Dhomhnaill 1990, 60–63;
translation by Michael Coady)

⌇

I sit here at my desk in Dublin, wondering why I am writing this. What is it I am trying to explain, and to whom? I have just got back from the local supermarket, where there was not a single word of Irish in sight, or a sound of it in earshot. I turn on the Irish-language radio station, Radio na Gaeltachta, a sort of lifeline. It is sometimes banal enough: a black-and-white dog has gone missing in Connemara; the results of last night's bingo in Na Doire Beaga are as follows. I keep feeling there is something very important I have to say, and that it has to do with Irish. Just because Irish is to all ostensible purposes almost invisible in suburban Dublin doesn't mean that it doesn't exist. Like yeast in bread, it is invisible, but it is what makes the culture rise. This is a difficult enough point to make in modern Ireland, where for many people it is the acme of sophistication and a kind of badge of modernity to deny any knowledge of Irish. Predatory capitalism, a sort of cultural law of the jungle, reigns supreme, and in such a schema Irish is superfluous, to say the least, if not downright retrograde. Love Irish as I may, I live in a maelstrom of other people's ambivalence and indifference to it, and it is a constant struggle to put it on the cultural menu. Not so long ago at a reception at the American Embassy, a woman asked me what I did (for a living). When informed that I write poetry in Irish, she asked what I wrote about. "Oh, the biggies," I retorted, "birth, death, and the most important thing in between, which is sex." "Oh," she said archly, "is there a word for sex in Irish?" I was so dumbfounded I was unable to answer her in proper time-tested Kerry fashion by asking her another question back, "Is there an Eskimo word for snow?" I remember a similar instance a few years ago where a woman journalist waltzed into my house to interview me and her first question was "Are you a Fascist?" Just because I write in Irish.

The question I ask myself now is how these women, who are about my own age, give or take a few years—definitely we could be considered the same generation—and like me grew up in Ireland about the same time, how on earth could we be so totally different? How is it that all of us, living as we do in Ireland, can be living in worlds that are so totally different? The fact that our family have been coming and going from this island for four generations now may have something to do with it. These women seemingly have a sense of ontological security that I sorely lack. They simply live here in Ireland, and for them their own reality is uncomplicatedly Irish, but as someone who has been displaced, both as an internal and an external emigrant, I have had to make my home not in Ireland but in a version of Irish which is not just a language but also a culture, a memory, and a fictional interaction with that memory. This is not without its plus sides—it gives me a freedom to invent what I want *Irish* to mean, and in doing so to change it. Not knowing whom I belong to—being too Irish for embassy hangers-on and journalists, too English for Jacsaí Shea—is the price I pay for the power to change the meanings of things and for the freedom to make those changes available to others without distinction of nationality, through poetry. I sometimes feel as a result that I carry a lot of emotional baggage, not all of it of my own making, but consisting of the tail ends of many displaced destinies that I have inherited down through the generations. I recently came across a story associated with Lady's Cross outside Dingle that I find deeply fascinating, as it seems to be the perfect description of my predicament. It is called "Fuíollach na gCeirtlíní," which I can maybe best translate as "The Leftovers of the Balls of Wool."

> There was this man coming home from Dingle one night and at the crossroads that they call Lady's Cross what did he see lying inside in the ditch but a tiny little itsy-bitsy bit of an old woman. She asked him to give her a hand up out of the ditch and he did. She asked him for the second hand up. "No, I will not," he said, "if you had half a mind to come out of that ditch I could have lifted you out already with only the one arm. What on earth is that weight on your back that is keeping you down in the ditch? Leave my hand go, or get up, one or the other." She said that while she was alive she had been a fuller's wife and, when her husband's clients had brought her wool to full, she had kept back the leftovers of the balls of wool and not returned them when the task was done, and her punishment now after death was to carry the leftovers of these balls of wool around on her back, and this was the weight that was keeping her down in the ditch. When the man woke up next morning, he noticed that the arm he had extended to help her was all bruised black and blue. He was thankful that he hadn't given her the second arm, or God only knows what might have happened to him.

The ball of wool is a common symbol in Irish folklore, especially in the hero-tale genre. There the hero or heroine is often handed a ball of wool which slips out of his or her hand and rolls ahead of them so fast (as the formulaic phrase goes) "that it catches up with the wind before it and the wind behind it does not catch up with it." Following this unreeling ball successfully leads the hero(ine) to their destiny, and so the unreturned balls of wool in the above story seem to me to symbolize the unredeemed, unlived, and, above all, unexpressed destinies of many generations before me, which for some reason I have been asked to carry. And a lot of these tangled balls and unreturned skeins are the result of many generations of emigration and displacement, especially on my mother's side.

Catherine Byron. Photograph by Maxine Beuret.

Catherine Byron

II Crypt

The first examination of conscience

There are bones
haunting the fridge
with mould on them like moss.
How many years now
since my carnivore days
when I picked the cage
of a chicken carcase clean?
Oh, and that pig's head
that I boiled for brawn
in a Scottish winter.
Remember how I needed
a brick to lid down the snout
when the boiling made the gristle
rear right up with the heat?
The brawn was clear and lovely
like a cache of garnet and pearls.
Never again, though. Never again.

The second examination of conscience

Eggs in a bucket
swimming in isinglass.
Whole eggs from the hens
the shells gone leathery as turtles',
whites gone all to water
yolk sacs slack and milky
so easily torn.
How I cashed in on their
mother-frenzy, my lovely
Rhode Island Red
Light Sussex cross
layers. From point of lay
to their moulting each Nov-
ember I forced them to be
egg-crazy, egg-a-day
wonders. I laid up
their overplus, stashed eggs
like oval ghosts in a pool
against their bald eclipse.
And all infertile: I'd
coq-au-vined long since
their solo cock of the coop.
Never again. I'll not
swallow any of that.
I have no stomach for it.

The third examination of conscience

When I bought the cleaver
at the butcher's suppliers
in the cold hinterland of East Kilbride
the man behind the counter
asked me quite straight
did I get on, like,

with my old man?
      Fine.

Oh, I knew then fine
what cleaving was:
to split with a blow
or to hold on tight.
A man and a woman
shall be one flesh.
Cleave thou only
unto him. One flesh.
         (from Byron, "Coffin. Crypt.
          Consumption." 2000, 7–8)

An Appetite for Fasting?

> A poem can't free us from the struggle for existence, but it can uncover desires
> and appetites buried under the accumulating emergencies of our lives, the fab-
> ricated wants and needs we have had urged on us, have accepted as our own.
>   —Adrienne Rich (1993, 12–13)

Ten years ago I was barefoot on a crowded island of penance, St. Patrick's Pur-
gatory on Lough Derg in County Donegal. It was a poem that had drawn me
there; not at all, I thought, my long-collapsed Catholic faith. Over in England
I had been trying to explain aspects of Seamus Heaney's sequence *Station Is-
land* (1984) to baffled fellow readers of his work. Like him, I had grown up
Catholic in Northern Ireland. Surely, friends said, I could tell them what he
was on about in this poem that sat so uncomprehended at the heart of his col-
lection of the same name. The more I read the sequence, the more I felt the
need to find answers to queries of my own. I wanted to be bodily in that place
to listen out for the female voices whose silences and absences had intrigued
me down the years in Heaney's previous work. In *Station Island* they had be-
come resonantly out of earshot, but unquestionably there. The words of an-
other poet nagged at me: "I do not know which to prefer, / . . . The
blackbird whistling / Or just after" (Stevens 1955, 93). I loved the Zen way
in which Wallace Stevens paired a sound with its shadow-silence, giving equal

weight to each. Heaney's comparable pairings in *Station Island,* of sound and its silence, presence and its air-held absence, lacked Stevens's purity. Their emptiness and voicelessness referred only to women, or to girl-children. His male ghosts might not be embraceable, but they could certainly speak.

I wanted to see whether, as a woman, and walking barefoot on the ancient sacred site of stone and water built over by more than a millennium of Christianity, I could hear the audible female silences, touch the palpable female absences so intriguingly implied in a sequence that was, amongst many other things, the autobiography of a male poet's soul. I was feeling both uneasy and optimistic about Heaney's recent work: he was a poet whose writing had long had an ambiguous gut-hold on me. There was so much that I recognized and felt affirmed by in his previous scenes from the complexities of growing up Catholic in rural Ulster. Why then my growing unease the more I reread this new work?

Station Island is Heaney's revisitation in dream-vision of an island that is peopled by ghosts from his boyhood and early manhood: an island that gives them back their (male) voices, at first affirming the poet, then arraigning him; increasingly self-reflexive. Of all those voices, the most difficult in every sense—for poet, for reader, for anyone involved in Ulster's trouble—is that of Francis Hughes, the second IRA man to die in the 1981 hunger strike in the prison of Long Kesh.[1] His aggressive passivity, his rejection of all nourishment, is particularly problematic for women, whether as witnesses to the historical "act" or as readers of Heaney's poem about him, the ninth in the twelve-poem sequence. At the dark heart of a pilgrimage that requires unusually harsh (for late twentieth-century Christians) fasting, and a complete removal from the rhythms and repasts of hearth and home, Heaney has the hunger striker, a very special sort of "fasting artist," holding center stage.

Before I went, physically, to St. Patrick's Purgatory on Station Island in remote Lough Derg[2]—and took off my shoes and socks for the three days and two nights in order both to comply with the penitential rubric of the pilgrim-

1. David Beresford's *Ten Men Dead: The Story of the 1981 Hunger Strike* (1987) gives a remarkably well-documented and contextualized account.

2. I went to St. Patrick's Purgatory 24 August 1987, rather late in the annual pilgrimage season, which runs from 1 June to 15 August. About eight-hundred fellow pilgrims arrived on the same day as me, and another thousand on the next. Each pilgrim spends three days and two nights on the island. During 1987 the total number exceeded thirty thousand pilgrims.

age and (more romantically) to sense the ancient stones and soil of the island through the bare soles of my feet, walking and circling before I set out for Donegal with Heaney's slim volume in my hands—I thought that the fasting would be the toughest part of my own "station." I couldn't imagine getting through the three days of that medieval hangover of a pilgrimage without the warmth and fullness and conviviality of meals. And afterwards, when I was re-living the whole experience in the months that it took to write the book *Out of Step* (Byron 1992b), it was the tenth chapter, the one that dealt with the im-plications of Francis Hughes's death from self-starvation, and the different "readings" of it that came from feminist, Catholic, historical, and political perspectives, that was the most anguishing to write. It was also, indeed had to be, the longest. And it was the chapter that, mysteriously, refused electronic transfer and had to be rekeyboarded at the publisher's and therefore proof-read by me word for word in the old, laborious way. All the other chapters/files on my disk transferred their data with sweet reasonableness.

I had mentioned in one of my writing seminars at the art school earlier that summer that I was going on a historic and penitential Irish pilgrimage at the beginning of August. I would be fasting for three days, I told my students, and walking round the circular remains of hermits' beehive cells on bare feet, night and day. Over the remaining weeks of the term, students kept coming up to me, always singly, and shyly offering their advice. "Oranges," said the first one to take me to one side. He was a mature student, a butcher who had left the meat trade to retrain as a fine artist. He saw himself as the reincarna-tion of Van Gogh, and specialized in abattoir studies in heavy impasto. "Take plenty of oranges with you for when you're over the fasting period. They'll get your gut working again like nothing else." My gut? Oddly enough, I was baf-fled by this first mention of one of fasting's possible consequences. "Yeah. It's being bunged up that's the problem every time for me. Getting things going again." It was the "every time" that intrigued me. It turned out that he fasted regularly, for forty-eight hours every four weeks. Just water, not even fruit juice. It was essential, he said, for his work. It cleared the creative imagination, freed it up, just as it cleared the body. Oh, and he was thinking of turning veg-etarian next.

Others came to me with similar stories of regular fasting, and a variety of tips. "Drink, like, gallons of water. It's a bit like a hangover, after," said a young woman whose sculptures were made of found detritus and beachcomb-ings. "You'll be on a high," said another. "Detoxification, that's what it is. It

simplifies everything. Better than tabs, or acid. Be prepared to go a bit wild."
A third suggested: "I'd take a packet of pure glucose with you, the lozenges,
you know—like you're allowed to take into exams. It's not really cheating if
they help you through a bad patch in the small hours. Chocolate now—that
would be cheating." This was all very practical, and apparently based on expe-
rience. It was only the fine artists who came with their know-how. The textile
design and silversmithing students were either ignorant of the benefits of fast-
ing or unforthcoming. The ceramics students, I knew, had their own secret
field of magic mushrooms in the outwoods, a location passed down to first
years every September in an initiation rite that was at least half-serious.

Could it be that the painters and sculptors were onto something? That
their creativity was reliably released or refreshed by a very regular, workaday
regime of one-, two-, three-day fasts? I liked the idea. Fasting as a way of wis-
dom, even of vision. Visions of Hell and Purgatory were, after all, what Station
Island had been famous for for centuries. I began to feel rather excited. Once
I was on my way to Station Island, on the St. Patrick's Purgatory service bus
from Dublin that carried thirty or so of us pilgrims northwest across the
bumpy, undistinguished midlands of Ireland, the fasting did not seem too dif-
ficult, as long as water was permitted. I'd been fasting from midnight. If you
are busy and focused, I thought, and nobody else around you is eating, fasting
isn't hard. Once we were on the island, one visit to the kitchen was allowed in
that first twenty-four hours for a grim snack of dry toast and black coffee or
tea. That too was fine. There were hundreds of pilgrims now on the tiny is-
land, and we were all in this together. And the *craic*,[3] as groups of us took our
turn at the long benches and refectory tables, was great. It was only when the
long night of the Vigil began, and we did circuit after circuit inside the basilica,
rosary responses, creeds, droned prayers without end, that I started to feel the
fast clenching my stomach. Even then it was surprisingly easy to dismiss the
discomfort. As that longest of nights went on, it was the loss of sleep and not
the fasting that became unbearable. The longer the spells in the basilica, the
more the bodies of the slouching pilgrims craved sleep, and gave in to it, mo-
mentarily. I saw people asleep where they stood, even where they walked. We
were kept going by the shove-and-crowd mind of this forced march that was
paced by prayer and response, prayer and response. On one level this made for
a very human solidarity, and the short breaks taken for a smoke, or even a game

3. Chat; conversation.

of cards in the night shelter, were welcome in their lack of sanctimony. Nothing—not the mantra-like communal chanting, not the hunger, not the deprivation of sleep, not even the wind blowing off the dark waters of Lough Derg—nothing brought a smidgen of illumination, or a glimpse of Hell.

During the longueurs of the second day, when it was even more difficult not to nod off in the thin sunshine, I read the poems of St. John of the Cross, and the autobiography of St. Teresa of Avila,[4] a couple of sensual mystics to inspire me, keep me going. But there was a hollowness in my heart that was to take me a long time to articulate. Perhaps, I thought—as I left the island on the third morning, with a profound sadness that I could not yet name—perhaps this pilgrimage has been too crowded, too cheerful, too watered down. Perhaps I was hoping for too much when I wanted to sense through my bare feet the pre-Christian sacredness of water and stone, the ancient female spirit of place? I came away with mixed feelings of personal failure and wounded feelings of good riddance. Ireland, country of my mother, and mother of me for my first seventeen years, was suddenly no longer haven or wellspring. Station Island had dealt me a body blow: my writing, my poetry in particular, came out of the matter of Ireland, its women's histories, its landscapes, its long losses through emigration.

I looked at the people sharing the great open boat that was taking us back across the lake to the mainland. Seven out of ten of my fellow pilgrims had been women, and this, I'd been told, was the norm. But I had found the island's voices and viewpoints to be entirely male, as much so in the Catholic liturgy as in Seamus Heaney's poem, though the emphases were, naturally, very different. The actual women I talked to on the island had many different takes on all this, but they accepted it, worked with it even in working against it. In the boat they were calling out to each other that we'd all be back the next year. The island had a hold on ye, sure enough. Not, I swore, on me—and I haven't been remotely tempted to go back, to either it or to my ex-faith. But when I left Ireland within the week, and for the first time ever was glad to do so, I felt as if there had been a death, or a divorce, deep inside me.

4. In Poem XI of *Station Island*, Heaney's pilgrim persona meets his confessor, "[r]eturned from Spain to our chapped wilderness," and is given as his "penance" the task of translating "something by Juan de la Cruz." Spain, and its spirituality in particular, has had a long connection with Irish Catholicism, and a special place in Heaney's own *bildungsroman*. See Peggy O'Brien's essay, "Lough Derg, Europe and Seamus Heaney" (P. O'Brien 1992–93).

Naming that grief took a long time. It is not fully encompassed yet, and it is only through writing that I can slowly, unevenly continue the process of grasping it. In the slow, painful retracing of the ground of Station Island as I wrote *Out Of Step,* I began to understand how much of my sorrow was anger. The book grew into a critical, historical, spiritual travelogue that was roped together by autobiography. Only by being completely open about the circumstances of my own barefoot reading of Heaney's sequence could I work out what I was so angry about. I needed to be there in the text, not to absent myself in the impersonality of "the author." Heaney had conjured up the ghost of James Joyce to welcome his pilgrim self off the island, to cheer him, and send him on his way. It was Annie Dillard and her *Pilgrim at Tinker Creek* (1976) that I held tight to, that wonderful journal of her year of walking, thinking, reading, and contemplation on the same circuit, the same ground.

As I wrote my way through the three days of my Irish pilgrimage, the realization dawned that the corner-of-the-eye women, the just-out-of-earshot women that I had gone in search of were not, really, the point. What was happening in Heaney's sequence as the poems darkened, and sectarian murders, bombs, then the hunger strike took center stage, was a progressive feminization of the male speakers in ways that became grotesque. Unwise passivity, victimhood embraced, a travesty of nurturing—it is a complex mix of manhandled myth, colonization's tics, and a religion whose ground rule is "offer it up." If Heaney were right, and the men of the nationalist community had become so unattractively feminized, where did the women come into it?

It was an extraordinary and painful vision of the nationalist dilemma. What I found so hard to understand or forgive was the way Heaney's pilgrim self, having revealed this horror, walked away from it. In the last three poems of the twelve he draws back from this cliff or fall, and with a little light penance is off and away, with James Joyce's blessing: " 'Let go, let fly, forget. / You've listened long enough. Now strike your note' " (Heaney 1984, *Station Island* XII, lines 29–30). Just like a man, I thought, my anger tipping me into my own sin of stereotyping. I thought I had at last named the reason for my earlier gut feeling that Station Island was seriously out of step with me, and I with it. Recently, though, it has been back haunting me in a different guise after a gap of several years.

⤳

I love food. Of all the writing I had hunted down about St. Patrick's Purgatory before I went, the story I most enjoyed was Sean O'Faolain's "Lovers of the Lake," where the two lovers drive off from their uneven "stations" on Lough Derg and right across Connemara, to fill the hours before midnight and enjoy the dinner that awaits the end of their fast: "These homing twelve o'clockers from Lough Derg are well known in every hotel all over the west of Ireland. Revelry is the reward of penance. The porter welcomed them as if they were heroes returned from a war. . . . Within two minutes they were at home with the crowd. The island might never have existed if the barmaid, who knew where they had come from, had not laughed: 'I suppose ye'll ate like lions?' " (O'Faolain 1981, 41–42). Yes, I thought, the whole point about fasting was the heightened pleasure that food and drink gave you after it was over. Well, not the whole point, not the Church's point—but sure, wouldn't you say grace, and mean it, for at least the next couple of meals?

In actuality my physical problem with the fasting required on St. Patrick's Purgatory had turned out to be trivial. (Yes, I did take that packet of glucose tablets, and yes, I chewed them slowly and gratefully at about 5 A.M. on the morning of the vigil, when my blood sugar was at its lowest.) My problem with the hunger striker's involuted voice and barren death at the heart of Heaney's poem had been a critical one: I would engage with it later, when I was writing it up. For me the forbidding of sleep—through the interminable night, on and on in the bright tedium of the second day—had been by far the greater penance, the harsher fleshly privation. In the long run, however, the shadow of fasting has been the darkest of all the shades that have haunted me from that double pilgrimage: the walking of my station on the island, and the subsequent walking of heart and mind through the writing of *Out of Step*.

It was years later that my colleague Sue Thomas, the novelist, said that she was sure that I had become a saint. I had to laugh. Sue, of all my friends, is the one most innocent of a Christian upbringing. I had been astonished and pleased that she had read *Out of Step,* and understood it so well. Much of its range of reference was unknown to her, but she is, after all, a science fiction writer, so I guess she is used to strange societal and belief structures. But me a saint? I felt sure she hadn't got any of her facts right. I had been ill. I had lost some weight, and now was living quite contentedly, on a nutritional supplement that gave me all I needed. The surgery I had undergone to alleviate the problem had, in fact, made it dramatically worse, but I was so relieved to have found at last a painless way of "eating" that I did not miss real eating at all. I was, nevertheless, a great oddity to the few who noticed that I never ate. New to ill health, as well as to this inability to eat normally, I found myself in another category: the recipient of etiologies and their corresponding systems of healing, both conventional and alternative.

In her last book, *Love's Work,* the philosopher Gillian Rose wrote of the reaction of friends and colleagues to the diagnosis of her ovarian cancer:

> I could compose a divan of divination, an anthology of etiologies:
> *Camille Paglia* (American author and media personality): "Nature's revenge on the ambitious, childless woman."
> *Braham Murray* (theatre director, my first cousin): "Your inspiration poisoned at source."
> *John Petty* (Provost of Coventry Cathedral and faith healer): "Transgenerational haunting and possession."
> *Ian Florian* (Principal, College of Traditional Acupuncture): "Imbalance of energies necessary for a woman to sustain success in the world."
> (Rose 1995, 77–78)

My illness was not life-threatening, yet it clearly made people think they should explain it, code it, find me a cure, a way back to normality. But I was feeling so much better on my ultrasimple regime that I was not myself engaged in seeking etiologies, or even a cure. I was finding surprising pleasures in vicarious, and even in virtual, eating. And the last thing I wanted was the label of saint.

Sue meant it, of course, in an almost value-free way, whereas for me it came laden with Christian baggage of suffering and self-sacrifice. Then her daughter Amber lent me a science fiction novel by an American professor of linguistics, Suzette Haden Elgin. In *The Judas Rose* (1987), Elgin describes women in a future period of worldwide famine rediscovering the possibility of living entirely on music. Monks and nuns had lived so frugally in the Middle Ages: perhaps the continual singing of plainchant had been a major contributor to their diet? In secret, her women linguists refine the skill of audiosynthesis and pass it on to the hungry people under the cover of music teaching.[5]

Not long after Sue had called me a saint I was one of several poets commissioned to write a long poem on the theme "Ghosts" for a performance at

---

5. Recently I came across an account of a Bengali woman saint, Giri Bala, "the woman yogi who never eats," a contented householder who was visited by Paramahansa Yogananda in 1935. She lived by a sort of spiritual photosynthesis, and by tuning in to "the hum of the Celestial Motor" (see Yogananda 1993, 524–53).

London's South Bank Centre.[6] For four long months I worked on one about a wife taking on the Orpheus role and venturing into the underworld in an attempt to win back her husband to the light. I kept returning to the myths of the Greek underworld in dissatisfaction. Persephone, Alcestis, Eurydice: so many women poets keep taking them on, rewriting them, but I could not work out why and how they kept nagging at the poet in me. Suddenly, ten days before the deadline, quite another poem began to arrive, and fast. I was back working on material I had long filed and forgotten, namely, my research into the St. Patrick's Purgatory of earlier centuries. Well-off pilgrims had paid to have a funeral mass said over them as they lay within an open coffin. Then the coffin was sealed in the subterranean cave of St. Patrick's making, and the pilgrim was entombed for ten days and nights, with only enough bread and water for barest survival. No wonder the place was renowned as one of the chief entrances to the underworld, already notorious in Dante's day. No wonder pilgrims in those days saw visions of Hell and Purgatory.[7]

My new poem was interested only in the mock funeral at first, not those infernal possibilities; then it opened into what became three "Examinations of Conscience." Fasting and abstinence from food became their (unwilled) focus. As soon as I had put this section together, and before I wrote the final one, I took Maud Ellmann's book *The Hunger Artists* (1993) down from my dusty Station Island bookshelf. The older I get the more I find that the way in which I read a once-familiar text is as mobile and unpredictable as my way of writing a new one. It was as though I were reading the opening words of its first chapter, "Autophagy," for the first time. They took my breath away: "A

6. My reading of "Coffin. Crypt. Consumption" was given at the Purcell Room on 13 December 1995, and recorded for transmission on BBC Radio 4 on Christmas Day 1996. The third "Examination of Conscience" was the inspiration for, and the central text in "Couple," a large (108 x 145cm) mixed-media work on two calfskins by artist-calligrapher Denis Brown. This work was commissioned from us both for the touring exhibition "Words Revealed," originated by the Midlands Arts Centre, Birmingham, in partnership with the Crafts Council of Ireland, for a two-year tour of Britain and Ireland in 1996–98.

7. The best-documented example of the false funeral is that of Raymond de Perilhos, a Knight of Rhodes and Chamberlain of Charles VI of France. In 1397, armed with a letter of safe conduct from Richard II (of England), he arrived at St. Patrick's Purgatory in the hope of seeing how his beloved late master, John I of Aragon, had fared in the next world. He claimed that the extreme lengths he had gone to had been rewarded—and he later made good political use of his professed visions. A detailed account of his adventures is given in Cunningham 1984.

few years ago a friend told me that he was going to a wake in Belfast for a woman who had been in a hunger strike in Armagh, the principal detention camp for female terrorists in Northern Ireland. She had survived the hunger strike, and had even been released from prison, but had died within the year of anorexia nervosa" (Ellmann 1993, 1).

What is the relationship between these two forms of self-starvation, so similar in their physical effects and yet so incommensurable in their meanings? I had known that women prisoners had been on hunger strike too but that the IRA command had excluded them from the high-profile strike of 1981. I had completely forgotten this story linking, so poignantly, the hunger strike with anorexia nervosa.

I had been very close to several sufferers of anorexia, still am, but I had not in my earlier reading of her book taken to heart Ellmann's extraordinary juxtaposition. She writes that her aim in writing it is "not to find the cause of self-starvation but to follow the adventures of its metaphors" (1993, 15). How I warmed to that disdain for etiologies as I read on. Starving, writing, imprisonment: it was an astonishing and scary ride. The third chapter, "Sarcophagy," transfixed me with its close reading of Clarissa's fictional self-starvation (in Samuel Richardson's 1740s novel) alongside the real-life self-starvation of the ten men in Long Kesh. She was writing of the apparent feminization of the men "in that their bodies were transformed into images of meanings rather than the instruments of acts." But there are also "fierce dissymmetries between the sexes. For the men imprisoned in the Kesh, hunger was a public and concerted enterprise, the corporeal expression of their . . . demands." Clarissa starves herself in private, "like the modern anorectic." Though a vigorous user of words, Clarissa "never articulates the reason for her hunger. . . . Word and flesh consume each other in her . . . inexorable quest for discarnation" (Ellmann 1993, 71–72).

The kernel of my three "Examination of Conscience" poems had been written a year earlier, for my closest poet friend, Gillie Griffin. I wrote about a fridge haunted by chicken bones and brawn—"fromage de tête." After I had written it, I knew it was for her. The woman in the poem vows never to eat meat again. It was only when placing the piece in this new context that I understood what I'd written, what I had given her. Gillie was not just a vegetarian. She had been anorectic years before, and still felt shadowed every day by anorectic habits of thought and feeling. That had not been in my conscious mind at all. It is strange how important forgetting is to writing. Like Keats, I feel uncomfortable about poetry that has designs on me—especially when it is my own.

The deadline was by now helpfully close. The final poem of my sequence turned out to be an invocation to Hades, not only as lord of the dead—though my first experience of serious illness was making me only too anxious to propitiate him—but principally as "prince of peristalsis, potholer extraordinaire," the guardian spirit of those more palpable underworlds: bowels and drains; more literally still, the camera eye of endoscopy. The title was a rush job: simply "Coffin. Crypt. Consumption."

I am content with all these odd juxtapositions, and decisions and compositions made under duress: I want to become more puzzled, less sure, the older I get. I want to be surprised as a reader, and even more as a rereader. I hope to surprise myself most of all in my writing of poetry. It was this poem's pressing deadline that late, late in the day let through some more of the ghosts I didn't see on Station Island. Prose is one way of journeying to understanding. Poetry can be a form of divination.

When *Out of Step* came out, many women—and some men—wondered why I had spent so much time and anguish over a man's text. I wondered too, and never more so than when I realized that that text had become spoiled for me precisely because it had, unwittingly, of course, forced me to read it as a woman first and foremost. I had to confront within myself the learned privileging of the male, so exquisitely inculcated in a Catholic girlhood in Ulster, and hardly shaken by years of being intellectually a feminist. *Station Island* acted on me, to its own detriment, in the way Adrienne Rich describes in the epigraph to this essay; or, more oddly, in the way Heaney's Joyce urges on his male pilgrim-self in *Station Island:* " 'Let go, let fly, forget. / You've listened long enough. Now strike your note.' "

As reader, as writer, I see that my task in this Vale of Soulmaking is to shuffle off the impedimenta of my "fabricated wants and needs." Now I am learning at gut level about hitherto unfamiliar disorder and dysfunction. No etiologies, please, no miracle cures. I want, in Ellmann's words, to follow the adventures of the metaphors.

Eithne Strong. Photograph by Patricia Boyle Haberstroh.

Eithne Strong

The Mahonys Observed

Does Mahony get an unfair deal like most only worse?
A man in chase of Truth, he never takes his full of rest
and Truth wears many masks exhausting him to find her face.

He never stops. His house is swarmed with torments
from his raw and truthwould heart. Only in heaven
will it be known, he said, finding his special Christmas

slippers in the garden pond, his new tie in the jam.
His wife, a sort of literate shrew, no helpmeet, complains:
All of my body's veins are near the surface; they clump

and knot in tumescence, excess of blood against contraction.
A shrew shrilly at his life's intention: Must I forever
play pretender, never state, for appearances' protection

that you have packed me with seed I never had the urge
to need? And must I halleluia for you who tyrannised
amicably my every year with salutary all-lovingness

which, oddly, never loved helping me on another way?
My plural womb engorged perennially against the sink;
my total energy to breeding went, to battered days'

➜

endeavour, nursing, patienting the chaos of the young.
If this were the full of Mahony's case . . . but is it
quite? Yes, she hacks at his adamantine moral legs

yet finally closes her most peculiar brand of balm
around his sapphire wounds, and so they jointly meet
the possible days, stubbornly greet untellable continuum.

(Strong 1993, 16–17)

Married to the Enemy

I was born into the bog country of West Limerick, province of Munster. 1923 was the year; therefore, my very young days coincided with the aftermath of centuries' colonization compounded by the civil war. The name of our locality was Glensharrold, or, in our native tongue, *Gleann na Searbh Úll,* which literally translates as the Glen of Sour Apples. The place-name is significant in its indication of the poverty—or what generation on generation must have considered poverty—of the soil. No sweet apples grew. In fact, no apple trees were commonly grown but, true, here and there one found a wild tree of little autumn sour, sour crab apples. The land about was considered meager, the holdings were small, privation was widespread. At the time, it was generally thought that bog country was mostly unproductive except of turf, a commodity more generally understood as peat, but never in our local parlance was such a term used. In reality, the ground could have been much improved for diversified crop growing by proper drainage and manuring. But the new Irish Free State, as it was then called, had few resources to help along funding for improvements.

On that scanty land all could be hard labor from dawn to dusk. Transport was by donkeys and ponies and occasionally by larger horses. Motorized vehicles were few and far between until the late thirties. Costs were high in the scale and context of the period. Unending work and poor return—that's how it mostly was on the land at our end of the parish. People helped each other by the custom of "coring"—an expression taken directly from the Gaelic expression *i gcomhar,* meaning "together," "along with"—and also that of the *meitheal,* or "helping group." Word got around when someone was about to need help drawing home the turf and hay, and people materialized as a matter of course on the day.

There were the poor, scraping along on a few rushy acres. Even poorer still were those who lived in county council cottages which each carried with it just a quarter acre of ground, certainly not enough to produce a year's sustenance of potatoes but perhaps enough grass—despite the crowding dock and rag-wort—to keep a goat or donkey. The majority of dwellings were roofed with rush thatch—rushes were certainly plentiful in the district. Some twenty miles eastwards, where flourished grain crops in the rich soil of the Golden Vale, was the very well-kept straw-thatched village of Adare built on the estate of the Earl of Dunraven. It was indeed pretty, a roses-round-the-door village like one of those I later knew in the Cotswolds but of which, in my youth, I knew nothing. Thatch of rush in our locality mostly signified poverty, too often going with mud walls, floors, damp. However, in a later decade such thatch was to become sentimentally endowed in the nostalgia of some emigrants, in the romantic unreality of certain tourists, and by the blow-ins of hippie waves from the late sixties into the early eighties.

The priests had immense power and influence in regard to the collective psyche. They represented the pervading dominance of the Irish brand of Roman Catholicism: the creed was narrow, darkly prohibitive of the body's delight—even simple embracing and kissing of offspring over four or so was affected, awkwardness in this regard prevailing. Although the sacred commandment forbade superstition —"I am the Lord thy God, thou shalt not have strange gods before me"—belief, in reality, was largely superstitious, latched as it was onto what could be called indigenous paganism, nourished on pishogues—*piseoga*, meaning witchcraft and lore pertaining thereto.

As to material wealth, I have referred only to the Catholic population. In our immediate radius of a couple of miles, only one Protestant survived. She was old, infirm, widow of the landlord's agent of the previous order of things in my youth safely past. It was clear she had more than was sufficient. This old lady lived in a house amidst trees on the side of a glen, Glenastar, wherein was a small but scenic waterfall which fell into a quite sizeable rock pool of brown bog water. The glensides, running for about a quarter of a mile, were thickly covered with ferns and bushes, among these last a preponderance of hazelnut. The house was of inoffensive dimensions but nevertheless it was big in comparison to most other dwellings about and of a handsomeness unique in the area. Whoever chose the site had chosen well.

This old woman, relic of the abominated landlord era, was well regarded, for her husband had been one of the more humane operators. She lived quite secluded with her long-standing personal English maid and employing a few local people to help with upkeep. One of these, in a very smart blue uniform inclusive of gold-braided cap, took her about when she occasionally issued in a highly polished but tastefully quiet-toned car. People respected her on several counts. She kept to herself, never meddling; her presence was, however, beneficial. Those periodic forays in the car were not always just constitutional outings for, crippled, remaining in the vehicle and via her chauffeur, she sometimes bestowed goods on the most needy. As well as this, all children in the district were welcome at her house every Christmas Eve to receive a present. Perhaps one of the most appreciated facets of her beneficence was passive: she made no objection whatever that the glen below her house—which was familiarly known, not as indicated in the ordnance map, but by her name, Yielding's Glen—was the haunt of summer courting and swimming in the pool below the waterfall.

In the entire parish there were only about seven Protestants including the easygoing clergyman. That he had a penchant for the bottle availed this parson something of an affection that would not so readily have prevailed towards a tipsily-inclined priest. These Protestants of no abrasive means—outside the parson, the others were modest farmers—melded unobtrusively with the general populace.

We arrive helplessly, not an iota of control over our conception. I could have been born into one of the county council cottages. I had cousins thus born whose circumstances were often dire. It so happened I was born to two primary schoolteachers. My father, inherently rural and happy to tip around in a kitchen garden, was yet not a natural turner of the soil in the dawn-to-dusk sense; he had inherited the fields and bogs of our property but was glad of his assured professional pay. Even with the very tight salaries of their time, teachers were considered comparatively comfortable. The children of teachers could go on to secondary level education, and third level if at all possible—this latter possibility depended on the size of the family. Usually the privilege of university education could be managed for only one.

As I grew up, I absorbed the values prevailing—a process of osmosis combined with unrelenting pedagogy. As to religious views, Roman Catholicism reigned unquestioned. The supreme value. By this our outlook was shaped. Respect for other religions was conceded verbally, but nevertheless we were to see ourselves lucky to have been born into the one true faith and not into any other form of religion or false thinking such as, for one, ignorant paganry. Looking back, one can see the paganry in all religions—but that was not yet for me. At school we learned something—simplifications—of our heritage of early proud myth and magic, of Saint Patrick and his legacy of Christianity which our monks in turn spread further, of the Danes, the Normans, the English and our long subjugation for seven centuries. To be Irish was wonderful. The Normans understood that and became more Irish than the Irish. The English had treated us abominably. We were going now to show ourselves a nation once again with our own language—intensive courses in the native tongue were instituted for the teaching profession—our culture generally, our money matters, making the most of ourselves.

Growing up, I came to feel males had the better part. While only just into his teens, my older brother was allowed privileges not granted to me, for example, freedom of movement. He was permitted to mingle in situations from which I was barred, go off alone to join his pals in the evening. I was still too young to appreciate that I, a girl, was being protected. Fiercely, I objected and got into deep trouble for being "disobedient, disrespectful." Full of resentment, I had to accept that boys were granted greater scope. Listening was an essential process of my day. Doing it, I learned much I would not be told directly. I learned of salaries and wages, how men got more than women for the same work, how women had to give up work if they married. Females had the lesser part in the general scheme of things. Impotently, silently, I raged at not being born a boy.

Not until the onset of puberty and the sprouting of breasts did I begin to think being a female was not all minus. Then there was the living embodiment of my mother. I recognized that in our family my mother was invariably the strong doer. Coming from the north, her people, so she believed, derived from the Scandinavians. She was fair, blue-eyed, but petite. A little woman, not physically very strong, married to a great, tall, broad-shouldered man, she was the unceasingly operative, innovative, positive quantity in the household in spite of all sorrows and setbacks. I was deeply attached to both parents and, at this distance, see that I carried, carry, them both in varying measures inside me and, although I have much experienced the—Celtic?—brooding, melancholic aloneness that so often I sensed and saw in my father and also something of his passivity, I believe that the unyielding tenacity of my mother in me is what has most helped me along in the stumbling times.

My parents avoided involvement in politics. It was a sensitive subject, treated gingerly. We children were enjoined not to meddle with any of that stuff and to keep a civil tongue in our heads concerning it. There was much we did not understand. The Treaty was never discussed in front of us. Not even when we questioned about the man, a small white bust of whom in military garb always occupied the central place over the hearth. We learned he was Michael Collins, ". . . a very fine brave man," but no more. We realized that in some way our parents' preference for the *Irish Independent* newspaper as against the *Irish Press* indicated some unexpressed leanings. Only much later did I come to see that their careful attitude in regard to politics derived from the civil war.

The dangers and rancors were very precariously near the surface in our district. Bitterness and hostilities could erupt into violence unpredictably. My father, while inclined to some testiness under stress, was largely a peaceable man, asking little of life beyond walking the wonderful open wild countryside for miles when not at his job of schoolmastering. My brother, three years my senior, had decided views charged with a venom which puzzled me. He was anti-British. Anyone showing partiality in any respect to the English was a *shoneen*—an appellation of contempt, from the Irish *seoinin,* meaning a copier of, a toady to, the British. In my brother's view, William Cosgrave and his "crowd" in top hat and tails were all *shoneens.*[1] We were indeed young at the time. This mental venom in my brother did not tally with his wave of the hand to Mrs. Yielding's chauffeur driving past, nor his unquestioning acceptance of the benefits going with Yielding's Glen—property still in the hands of a representative of the traditional enemy—where he went fishing and swimming all summer. Nor did it tally with his easy response to Parson Sweeney's droll chatting. The parson, with his accent, sounded thoroughly British; his children were being educated in England. I did not yet know how to formulate all the queries arising out of much anomaly.

Anomalies abounded. Yes, much I did not understand. Abstractions were not part of our daily life. The edicts for thinking and living were delivered from the pulpit, unquestioningly agreed upon. To adopt any other philosophy was vile heresy. Love thy neighbor. Thou shalt not kill. Sacred commandments dutifully learned. Why then did Catholics—people of the supreme religion—kill one another in a tragic civil war? No one would tell me.

1. Favoring English over Irish styles, attitudes, values.

I repeat, much I did not understand. I knew that to be Irish was wonderful. I loved the Irish language but also the local vernacular, a kind of English rich in individual Irish words, in Irish language locutions and idioms and, as well as these, in locutions which were direct translations from the original Irish. With a passion I loved my country which for me was not really the larger island of Ireland—I had as yet traveled scarcely more than fifty or so miles in any direction—but that mountainy, boggy part of West Limerick where I was born. I was full of romanticism about our heroes. While rebellious, I was strongest in favor of those who advocated constitutional methods—O'Connell, Michael Davitt. Yet, again, the men of 1916 were heroes. *Sinn Féin* — We, Ourselves—one of their mottoes. I understood "ourselves" here to signify no dependence on England: we, the Irish, on our own impetus. In the 1930s we were supposed to be managing by ourselves alone, yet there was not enough to feed and clothe all the people. The Famine years and after, people went in shoals to America because of the mishandling of our country by England. Now a decade after our achieving independence, the people in hundreds were of necessity still leaving for jobs—this time mostly to England. In fact, the thirties were times of economic stress and unemployment worldwide, but even so the Irish left for England as though for something better. Marginally, it could be.

➵

Putting words down on paper—from incipient sentences—that was a real pleasure to me. I somehow got the notion of becoming a writer. I had no idea how to go about it, just vaguely believed I would find out. But to start with I was writing little paragraphs in the manner of Zane Grey. Think of the incongruity: the Irish bog landscape and its way of life, the only material of which I had close experience, scarcely equated with the other Wild West. However, I was about eight or nine. That was when the idea first flashed. It never really fizzled out but seemed to get a further hold when, at age fifteen, I was fortunate in having a particular teacher in boarding school. There was something of an aura of mystery to her: a nun, a convert, it was rumored, who had been reared in England, but she appeared invincibly private, so no one really knew. Her accent was English, identifiable with that of BBC newscasters. The only inkling we ever got was that now and then, to substantiate some point of view delivered to us in class, she would impersonally, enigmatically say, "I know. I've had experience." Certainly and astonishingly in a convent of the 1930s, as I realized only in retrospect, she was a person of greater mental flexibility than

I had yet encountered, with a consequently wide and stimulating appreciation of such literature as we covered in our year with her.

Her insights into and sensitive explorations of texts stirred further writing notions in me. A pity her tuition was in English only. She was special. But I have only gratitude for the teaching I was lucky enough to get in that school. With years and hindsight I can now forgive the narrowly constricting aspects of the religious area—nowhere in the country at that time, unless by near-miracle, would a student in a school run by religious find anything different. Although I was to move away from the damaging narrowness, I would not wish to move from much useful self-discipline I got, nor some abiding principles.

While intensely Irish insofar as I understood what that might mean—born Irish, deep love of my Irish parents, the homeland, the tongue, loyalty to ancient identity as heard and read of, loyalty to the Roman Catholic religion—from quite a young age I was aware of outward urges, away from the shores, urges often strong enough to be called longings. I had an appetite for Europe, all faraway places, a craving for experience to include other peoples, their thinking—the territory of mind had a singular attraction—and culture. Going to Dublin was a step in the direction of wider vistas. Although I was eligible for entry to University College, there were no scholarships to it from my county of Limerick. What was possible from family resources to meet a university course went to cover that of my brother, now a medical student. I did not grudge him, but the wish to encompass ever more knowledge and experience of realms abroad did not relinquish its gnawings. Horizons as I viewed them from my desk in the civil service were not promising, but I was thankful to be earning, to be able to spare my parents my upkeep—in that, too, I had an advantage on my brother, although by this stage I had mostly left behind the sibling rivalry of previous times.

I was writing private little bits of this and that in both languages. Without any doubt, in my case, involvement of the heart was a determining factor as to whether I was moved to write in Irish or in English. Once a member of *Craobh na hAiséirighe*—the branch of *Conradh* [2] I joined—I became freshly stimulated to attempt more work in Irish. I was much drawn to a particular member who, I considered, was an intellectual. It was this aspect of him which most interested me. My rearing did not predispose me to unmaidenly forwardness—in that upbringing one did not even think of the term *sex*. I believe

2. Organizations devoted to the study and preservation of Irish language and culture.

I had never heard it except as a term to differentiate gender. All veerings of thought in that direction were potentially fatal.

It was indeed encouraging when, without any changes whatever, he published a few poems in Irish of mine in the Irish language magazine *An Glór,* which he edited. The poems, I concluded, must have had some small worth, for surely I had no reason to imagine they appeared in print out of his partiality to me. Our meetings at this time were at the level of a kind of joking literary chat. In it might have been some indications of the kind of development I thought I wanted—a gradual intellectual interchange leading to some elusive, delicious intimacy. But subsequently, and altogether unexpectedly, things happened which very rapidly distanced me from the *Craobh.* My favorite member I saw only once afterwards and that was to explain some of the reasons which interfered with my continuing activity there. Among the reasons was a political turn in the *Craobh* with which I disagreed; another—and chief—was that a figure of much significance had suddenly come into my life who greatly absorbed my attention. My love of the Irish language was forever, I insisted to my literary friend, but new directions for me made our further meeting unlikely. A lifetime passed and he was buried before I heard from someone who claimed to know that, yes, he had indeed been *i ngrá* (in love) with me.

I sometimes, in hindsight, wonder about all this. It might seem we had been ready for each other but some invisibles were at work to separate our paths. Mine was to begin a quite unforeseen direction from the day fate decreed I met a particular man of the breed traditionally enemy—English, someone with whom I was quickly to discover I could share similar proclivities. I had not envisaged marrying young. My early vague plans had to do with consolidating writing ground and possibly marrying around age thirty. But I met Rupert Strong when I was just nineteen. A period of intense emotional experience followed, a period of very powerful tensions between loyalties. The divide between us was at once huge and nothing. In the larger perspective we complemented each other. Within six weeks we had pledged ourselves to marry.

On his father's side, Rupert Strong's upper-class family was traceable to twelfth-century soldiers and landowners—Anglo-Norman of the ruling class. On his mother's side there was Scottish-Bruce blood but also a complex blend of European strains, including Russian and German Jewish. Linking with this man profoundly influenced my life thenceforward. Indeed, Rupert Strong was a new, absorbing kind of animal in my ken. We found we had the writing bent in common. His reaction to some work of mine he had asked for was spontaneously warm, and I was much gratified—after all, was he not twelve years older, experienced, well-read? Always thirsty for praise, I lapped it up as it came. But he was also discriminating, advising here and there, and then—almost incredibly but most pleasantly boosting—he asked my advice on work of his. My self-confidence, always a very needy area, was being fed. And there was more.

Because of our joint interest in writing, Rupert Strong, with a few others, like-minded, chief among them Jonathan Hanaghan, became instrumental in bringing out a number of poetry quartos. I was one of the few who helped to fundraise for these and sell them, going from door to door around Foxrock and other, it was hoped, likely areas—that is to say, places with an aura of money that suggested possible interest in cultural activities in those days of war. Although Ireland was neutral, the war of course affected the country in so many ways. Good quality paper was difficult to find but we managed that. Established artists —Sean Keating, Jack B. Yeats, Sean O'Sullivan, Harry Kernoff—were engaged for artwork. Solicited poetry from well-known names, as well as unsolicited from emergent writers, appeared in the quartos: among others were Charles Acton, Leslie Daekin, Lord Dunsany, Herbert Read, Henry Treece, Alex Comfort, Roy McFadden, Maurice Craig, Robert Greacen, Valentin Iremonger. Some of mine were in them. I was the merest but immensely keen beginner in all of these proceedings. I was learning much fast. I did not like the fundraising but was committed. Money was always scarce. The publishing venture was named the Runa Press and, subsequent to its tentative start, it included other areas and remained in dogged, impecunious existence for nearly half a century.

We, the few giving sporadic time to the Runa Press, were surprised one evening by the arrival amongst us of a big-framed man who looked to be in his thirties, perhaps. What I noticed first about him were his charged limbs which jerked about as he talked, his loose clothes and their air of having been thrown on, the thick white woolen socks. He had heard of us, he said. He laughed at the idea, as much as to say "Make what you like of that." Laughing was part of his bigness; while it rollicked he threw his head back, his dark-framed spectacles jogging on the bridge of his nose the while. Had we any chance of work for him? he wanted to know. We explained—that is, the others did, for I was too new for that—the threadbareness of finances. But of course if he wanted to volunteer. . . . He howled in an excess of ridicule at the idea. But he stayed on a while, and having watched and delivered some gossip current amidst the

Dublin literati and bellowed some further laughter at that, he left us in amity. And that was Paddy Kavanagh, not so much further in the future to be known across continents as Patrick Kavanagh, worthy poet. Somewhere again in those early days when we speculated about the viability of other publishing possibilities, there materialized in our gathering room another long man, more slender and of swarthy good looks, tentatively nosing out the ground in our regard. He seemed guarded. Perhaps we were disappointing, if evidence of prosperity he expected. Over the years we were to have further productive dealings with this man, for he was Liam Miller, later founder of the Dolmen Press.

But why was Rupert in Ireland at all? He was already here a year when World War II broke out. He had come furnished with several introductions from well-placed connections in England. Attitudes to him ranged. To some—remnants of the previous ascendancy, he was suspect as not having stayed in the army to fight for England. Was he not a skulker, a shirker of responsibility to his motherland, plain coward? To others—of professional clout, orthodoxy, establishment—he was further suspect because of persisting in allying himself with the ideas and outlook of a practitioner of something quite new in Ireland, a matter which, in Europe and America, variously generated controversy, ardent endorsement, sneers, outright dismissal—all of these. The something was psychoanalysis. The particular practitioner in question was Jonathan Hanaghan. It was because of him, whom he had heard speak, with whom he had conferred in England, that Rupert Strong had come to Ireland. It was there Jonathan Hanaghan—of Scottish-Irish derivation but a British citizen, reared in the Church of England, married to an Irish Quaker wife—lived and worked. He was a powerful personality fueled by an endlessly probing intellect and vast energy. While eclectic in his study of the mind, he found Freud's the most comprehensive approach. He used this with modifications and insights he believed applied. Unlike Freud, he was not atheist but believer in a Deity. However, it is also true that he was perpetually open-minded, evolving, adaptive.

Liaison with Rupert meant, for me, much interaction of ideas. We were equally curious one about the other. I did not feel his wanting to know every aspect, move, even thought of my life, to be intrusive; rather, I felt it to be for closeness and understanding. Much bridging had to be done. There were great divergences in our backgrounds. I was acutely conscious of being raw, a novice. Very unsure, I greatly wished I could have been able to impress him with spectacular achievement. But what had I to show beyond the usual physical attributes of a budded virgin? The mental wares were, I feared, meager. I showed off from my little store—that is to say, I trotted out some myth and folklore of the ancient Irish tradition. I made good use of my involvement with the Irish language, brought him to meet some of my friends from *Craobh na hAiséirighe,* who politely switched to English in deference to his total ignorance of the country's tongue. He said he wished he could pick it up but knew he never would—life was too packed for him to hope to acquire new tongues. Indeed, he gave to understand in that terse, taut, yet quiet way he sometimes had, he wished he could. He was a citizen of the world, he said, and hoped to have something to do with developing better understanding between people worldwide.

In Dublin the group of people with whom he had most in common were those interested in the views of Jonathan Hanaghan. We all met regularly, the world of ideas, of attempting to relate ideas to practicalities, engaging us. More than ever I listened now and read. Read. Henceforth, wide-ranging reading material was always to be available to me and I devoured. The world of ideas, the opening up of mind: this was of enormous significance, meaning for me a radical swing of mental energy, a refocusing upon an area urgent parts of which we had been enjoined to seal up from first "use of reason." This last was a phrase with which we as children were familiarized from the age of six or so in preparation for First Holy Communion. Linking with what the majority in my country would call the traditional enemy, I found myself becoming at variance with many restrictive aspects of my previous conditioning. From the point where I linked with him, I was to counter much that previously I had never questioned. Going with the opening up of new mental territory were attempts to make actual some principles—experiments in living towards, it was to be hoped, the betterment of coexistence.

I brought Rupert to meet my family. They liked him, even the older brother who scorned the Brits. And it was astonishing to me that he should be thus disposed to this Englishman of the class he especially abhorred, with their imprint of destruction left indelibly on our history. The fact that my brother's initial response was positive underlined for me further how Rupert Strong must have become something other than his class demanded. When I took him around to visit some of the local people in Glensharrold, shyness was on both sides, but they eased towards one another, for there he was, like one of themselves, in his mud-spattered clothes—he had cycled the latter part of the journey down through rain and potholes—and there I was beside him, barefoot, for that was how I loved to be since childhood, in all manner of summer weather. His accent of course could have been for the people a distancing factor, but he was quietly spoken, with none of the stridency of the overlords of hated race memory. It was a good time, that first visit of his to our Glen of Sour Apples. Yet it was to be a very long, long, pain-fraught stretch before another such would occur, for all was to alter. My parents were deeply distressed when, in a genuine endeavor to meet the demands for conversion to Roman Catholicism so as to marry me, he found he could not in all sincerity do this. The fact that we persisted with our plans to marry resulted in painful schism which took many many years to heal. For a Catholic Irish girl, in the 1940s, to behave as I did was a terrible grief to her parents, who saw her plunged in the inexorable hell of the Church's teaching.

Schism was not what Rupert Strong wished. True, he had broken with almost all of his background while at heart remaining entirely loyal to certain emotional ties: love of his widowed mother and family—who considered him a puzzle, to say the least; love of certain phrases of some Church of England hymns, biblical snippets reminiscent of his dead father who had been a clergyman. Was there not something picaresque in his behavior, with its unpredictable course, queried his family? And yes, their confusion in this regard was understandable, for his trial and error had led him into his thirties before he decided with total conviction what he wanted to do, and that was to ally himself with the dedication of healing. From this time on, his whole *raison d'être* was to be healing—of the person, primarily, and thence outward. His inspiration—yes, that is the accurate term—in this respect was, of course, the thinking and living of Jonathan Hanaghan.

He had many ideological tussles with Hanaghan: such threshing out of matters was frequent in our circle, and that was healthy since the goal was positive. I had met nobody hitherto with Hanaghan's different approach to healing. What purported to be salutary tenets had been delivered to me from my first cognizant hearing. We had been told our religion was built on the loving, world-embracing, all-forgiving Christ. In reality, there could be wide discrepancy between fine principles and practices. At the time I met Rupert Strong, I did not know enough to be critical of that aspect of the Church I was reared in, although it had troubled me that the bishop in the diocese where I was educated lived in a great palace of a place—that was the actual designation: "the bishop's palace"—while round about there were hovels aplenty. The dark things in the religion were what had frightened and oppressed my growing years. The concepts all having to do with the Sixth Commandment, with their denial of the body, their conveying of the loathesomeness of sexual parts, the appalling punishment meted out to any unconfessed, unrepented, bodily explorations, even any thinking about such—all these had certainly had a profoundly negative, even sometimes crippling, effect on me.

The perspective of Rupert Strong was totally different. The body in totality was for celebration. The complexity of mind was for opening up, kept accessible to everything conceivable. One had the right of individual selection and decision. One's conscience was not to be controlled by shriveling pronouncements from pulpits or other points of domination. It was important to be able to explore, weigh the contrarieties—Blake had said "There can be no progression without contrarieties"—the ambivalences which make up creation, wherein everything contains its own opposite. Start with the self. Self-knowledge certainly ought to be a first aim: frank scrutiny of motive, of the countless occasions of conflict, tensions in the self; and then between the self and society, which is composed of other selves. I felt the perspective to be right.

Ours was a partnership of tensions. These led sometimes to storms: I was the stormer. But primarily we aimed—while not denying the tensions—to contain them so as not to crash irrevocably into the destructiveness of hurricanes: I was the potential hurricane crack; Rupert was pacifist—at some cost, including expenditure of great energy in sustained will.

He had been slighted, castigated for having left his army training years before coming to Ireland and for having refused to return to England to enlist for World War II. His pacifism was a larger application of a personal attitude: again, start with the self. He did not agree with allowing interpersonal rancors to fester, doing increasing damage. Encountering causes at person-to-person level and searching out how to resolve them—that was his way. This, again, was a new approach for me to live with. Previously, it seemed to me, people, including myself, often did not know what to do about difficult feelings and interreactions. We might try to evade any frank facing of them with a view to peace, or might break out in violent rowing that led to no solution. Ireland was officially neutral in World War II but, of course, one found quite a lot of the attitude that England's difficulty was Ireland's opportunity or that, at any Axis advance, the English had it coming to them. My parents had deplored all war yet, even so, various entrenched bitternesses with different relatives and certain neighbors manifested their vicious persistence in them time to time. My older brother was avowedly warlike. I had continued to encounter evidence of the scars and divisive effects of the civil war in my daily living: in our locality in West Limerick, in boarding school, in the civil service, in *Craobh na hAiséirighe*. Personal and interfamilial animosities, grudges, vendettas abounded in my home district and in any other social context I knew.

Out of the tensions writing issued. I firmly hold that no writing of conviction may happen without the compelling power of tension—lived through, maybe come to terms with, even surmounted. I suppose I write out of the deep which itself connects with the rest of humanity via, maybe, reverberations of lunacy, ecstasy, or plain quiet desperation and, of course, humor. Posturing I dread to discover in myself—I have been guilty of it through the years. May it be forgiven when understood to be the mark of insecurity.

I might have gone on to write much more in the Irish language. Here I encountered difficulties. I certainly knew conflict and tension regarding the language, having joined my life with Rupert. Other people to whom the language was deeply important have not allowed marriage to a non-Irish partner to interfere with the use of the language in the household. I wished to use it with my children but became discouraged. There were considerable pressures in those early years: a combination of factors was at work, having to do, among other things, with finances, domicile, schools. We were not well-off. In theory, the national school as an educational venue should answer that difficulty. But national schools were either strongly Catholic or Protestant—the latter fewer in number because of a smaller catchment. We thought of outlook before language in reference to schools. Neither of us wished our children schooled in the outlook of either denomination. The school we availed of was fee-paying and Church of Ireland but, we hoped, less parochially and ethically confined. A great-aunt, refugee from Germany in England, subsidized us in the matter of fees. Sadly, the Irish language was given scant attention in the school curriculum. To persist in my own private tuition was beyond my energy.

We lived experimentally in a communal venture. Those involved were of varying backgrounds. No one amongst them knew any Irish. One of the main goals of the venture was the resolving of barriers, not their creation. My husband, open-minded and citizen of the world as he was, would have liked to know Irish as much as he knew French and German but did not see space for doing this in his crowded day, and he admitted feeling somewhat fenced-off in the matter of his children speaking a language he would not know. There were enough complications to our marriage without that. Since linking with him, I had many times of feeling that I could be seen as *cúl le cine*—retrograde, betrayer of my roots—and the time of deciding about this issue of the Irish language for my children was indeed one of them. But in my heart I was not retrograde. Neither did I regret the marriage. We had many babies: a great deal to be said for a mate who, to help out, would willingly take on any activity of his wife's which he could handle, including the washing and hanging out of babies' napkins—disposables were in the future. Facetious as to our bond? Not quite: a nonromantic but entirely solid ground of reasoning and, without saying, there were uncountable other reasons for our durability.

How was my writing going? On little slips of paper were often jotted ideas as they sprang in the midst of imperative tasks. The slips got thrust into some drawer, to be worked on, I hoped, at a future point. That point frequently had to wait a long period, years sometimes. I was quite certain the children—in all, there would be nine—were my priority. The query surely arises: Why so many of them? Well, neither of us took to the notion of what we considered—perhaps idealistically?—artificial birth control: there were fears of impairment of spontaneous joy, of carcinogenic side effects. So what was left as preventive but to curb fleshly appetites or to endeavor to abide by what was known as the rhythm? Neither of us was good in restraining delights of fleshly rioting, and the rhythm quite simply did not work for me. Everything carries its price. The little babies, poor little scraps, did not ask to be born—one with brain damage. Clearly my first responsibility was to them.

Never once in the packed years did I relinquish the idea that I was born to write. Admittedly, I knew times of discouragement at the paucity of opportunity. I knew frustration in this regard, impotence, fierce resentment. I raged at my own capitulation to what I sometimes saw as the tyranny of the orgasm. And there were the babies, the hapless outcome. I could have been other: the restrained, removed female of nunly abstention I used to imagine in times of convent school spiritual yearnings towards "purity." I could have been a creature of structured life-plan with all energies coolly directed to strategies calculated how best to propel me to eminence in record time. But, in reality, there I was what I was. From passions, involvements, muddlings, unending strivings at the behest of conscience, from these and more arose my writing.

Experiences continued to expand. Our time of communal living was not lucrative but was dense in texture; rich, indeed, not excluding weeds and tares. Along with the core residents in the house, under the roof might also sleep, at a meal might also dine, transient folk including Jews, Germans, Japanese, Poles, Africans, Indians, and so on. Some forward-looking priests from Maynooth broke bread with us and engaged in prolonged discussion. These were in the days before Pope John XXIII, as far as I remember. One of them was to become archbishop of Dublin. Flawed, sometimes self-important in our unredemption, of course we fell short of ideals: money was short, tempers often so, energy also. But the fundamental goals, if on occasion misted over, were there; and the whole was an advance on civil war, on the atrocities of Auschwitz, Treblinka, Belsen, Hiroshima, Nagasaki. As far as I know, the venture was unique in Ireland at that point.

While we lived there, healing with my people at last blessedly occurred to the extent that my parents felt they could come and meet those whom my mother had previously denounced as "godless pagans." In the difficult years since the rift, some letters had been exchanged. Early in that time a letter came from my father, who normally eschewed all but necessary official correspondence to do with his work as teacher and matters of the land. His letter was couched in stiff phraseology such as he would never use in the rhythms of everyday speech. In remote formal language he exhorted me to return to my faith, to put from me the obstacles that stood in the way of my doing this. He spoke of the grave stress under which my conduct placed my mother and him, of the scandal I was to my brothers—"if thy eye offend, pluck it out" was the tone and inference if not explicitly said. The very fact that a letter at all had come from him told me, as much as did its content, the gravity of their plight regarding me. I replied as best I knew, saying—uselessly, I feared—that I cared about them all, although it might not seem so, but that I had to do things this way. It was the only letter I got from him in all the years of separation. I had continued to write to them at intervals, brief little notes just to try to show I had not cut myself off, to give accounts of doings around us, to even talk of my children, who were understood by my parents as being in the sad state of Limbo, not having received Baptism in the Catholic Church. This was of no avail, so I did it only in the most peripheral way, covering a little space to which to append my unfailing ending of "Love, Ettie"—the familial pet name.

My mother's replies at first were full of impassioned outrage and pleading. After a while they became brief and curt. Then came her news that she was coming for a few days to Dublin, alone and by train, on some business. She asked to meet me in a café. She would not come to the place where we lived, it being tainted with heretical modes of practice. I had not told her of the birth of my first child, much though I longed for her to be near me in the event, to share in the celebration. I had feared the birth would set up renewed pressure, this time to insist the child should be baptized a Catholic. Our meeting was understandably restrained. I told her of the baby. Her reaction was one of shock: her entire face and neck were instantly suffused in a frightening red flush, and I felt in deepest degree guilty at her fearful distress. Her attempt at some release from it was—as I had envisaged—to focus at once on the matter of Baptism. The next day I wheeled the little month-old child in the pram for her to see. A beautiful little girl, she won instantly the intrinsically womanly heart of her grandmother. But once returned to Glensharrold, my mother recommenced urgent implorings for me to do "the right thing." How could I have allowed the lovely little soul to dwell in the danger of Limbo for a whole month, she asked, for a countless time. I did not need reminding that Catholic teaching required Baptism as near as possible to births so as to eliminate the ir-revocability of Limbo. To try to say I thought differently about this now was only to bleed wounds afresh.

By the time my parents finally came to visit us in the communal situation, I had my fourth child. My father was one of those who find it difficult to be socially at ease except with a small number of closely known relatives and a few colleagues. The home setting, solitariness in the bogs and wilds of West Lim-erick—that was his natural habitat. For him, this first meeting and mingling with the heterogeneous group where we lived was a severe trial. That he stood it was witness to a profound and painful effort, spiritually and physically. He was looking older and worn. I knew I was a factor in his aged appearance and was both ashamed and helpless about it. A late and nervous driver, he had driven in the modest little Ford what for him was an unprecedented journey. My mother was a natural socializer and very quickly adapted to the setting.

The almost incredible instance of their coming had risen through the workings of a Jesuit cousin on holiday from responsibilities in Canada. Highly intelligent, sophisticated, urbane, diplomatic, he had visited us, talked to Jonathan Hanaghan, Rupert, and several others; and then he and I, alone, spoke at length about the whole religious and parental issue. I found him a person of cultivation and breadth; indeed, delightful. Afterwards, he had eaten with all of us, then departed for Glensharrold, where he achieved a remarkable change in the thinking of my parents. Thence the miracle of reconciliation.

As children we had been taught tolerance for other people's religions. The sacred and iron rule that was never to be broken was the forsaking of Catholi-cism. I had broken it. Hence the schism maintained so long by my parents. It was gravely wounding to us all but, in their lights, this was what had to be done to mark the wrongness of their daughter. My bonding with the traditional enemy had brought this about but then, ultimately, it meant my mother's mingling delightedly with the range of people constantly moving in and out of our circle. Several times I found her engrossed, exchanging views with African, Jewish, Swedish, or whatever friends happened to be around, on customs, ways of life relating to religious, domestic, and other procedures. I could see my father, too, now taking some relish in the flux, although he was more shy, less vocal.

In time we had to leave our communal setting, the property being officially requisitioned for building purposes. But in our new phase of existence, in the Strong home, the concept of inclusion was still with us and, in Rupert's lifetime, people of varying races came and went continually.

With Rupert's moral backing, it was settled that I took a degree: a spoke in the future. I arranged the finances for it through a bank loan. This was midlife for me: a particularly challenging juncture at which to do such a thing. I had worries about the family, naturally: was I letting them down being away so much at lectures, in libraries? Worries about the minutiae concerning the routine of my brain-damaged child. Structure was now of extreme importance, so I had to plan rigorously. Energy was unrelentingly demanded. However, all being grist, I continued writing a certain amount of what I suppose must be called creative output—poetry and also the odd short story—as distinct from papers of the academic genre, which were a heavy commitment at this time. My course meant renewed engagement with the Irish language, and this was a joy. *Sinn Féin*—We, Ourselves—motto of my early heroes: I had come to see that in a salutary way it could be applied in the singular: *mé féin*—I, myself. It was very much that *I*—by myself—in this belated academic excursion. A lot of the time I felt greatly lonely but recognized that no experience need be wasted— all is grist. From such inner scrutiny I was to see that within *mé féin*—me, myself—could be found and tapped a source of fortitude, enough to stabilize myself and, with grace, reach out to evoke that in other beings. None of it came easily but, as far as I was concerned, it became a fundamental process.

Have I regrets? Many. But, in regard to the particular Englishman, another human flawed as myself, none. In very considered retrospect, I am convinced: married to the traditional enemy, that Englishman, I have grown to know he was as sincere a striver as I might ever come across—and that is taking into account all Irishmen because, starting with himself, the basis of his living was the aspiring to overcome root causes in human makeup of divisions, barriers to universal amity. He believed in those hard things, forgiving and renewal.

Eavan Boland. Photograph by the Irish Times.
Courtesy of W. W. Norton.

Eavan Boland

From **Anna Liffey**

An ageing woman
Finds no shelter in language.
She finds instead
Single words she once loved
Such as "summer" and "yellow"
And "sexual" and "ready"
Have suddenly become dwellings
For someone else—
Rooms and a roof under which someone else
Is welcome, not her. Tell me,
Anna Liffey,
Spirit of water,
Spirit of place,
How is it on this
Rainy Autumn night
As the Irish sea takes
The names you made, the names
You bestowed, and gives you back
Only wordlessness?

Autumn rain is
Scattering and dripping
From car-ports

And clipped hedges.
The gutters are full.

When I came here
I had neither
Children nor country.
The trees were arms.
The hills were dreams.

I was free
To imagine a spirit
In the blues and greens,
The hills and fogs
Of a small city.

My children were born.
My country took hold of me.
A vision in a brick house.
Is it only love
That makes a place?

I feel it change.
My children are
Growing up, getting older.
My country holds on
To its own pain.

I turn off
The harsh yellow
Porch light and
Stand in the hall.
Where is home now?

Follow the rain
Out to the Dublin hills.
Let it become the river.

Let the spirit of place be
A lost soul again.

In the end
It will not matter
That I was a woman. I am sure of it.
The body is a source. Nothing more.
There is a time for it. There is a certainty
About the way it seeks its own dissolution.
Consider rivers.
They are always en route to
Their own nothingness. From the first moment
They are going home. And so
When language cannot do it for us,
Cannot make us know love will not diminish us,
There are these phrases
Of the ocean
To console us.
Particular and unafraid of their completion.
In the end
Everything that burdened and distinguished me
Will be lost in this:
I was a voice.

(Boland 1994, 44–46)

The Irish Woman Poet: Her Place in Irish Literature

1

My subject is the woman poet and the national literature of Ireland.[1] It may well seem—with such a subject—that my emphasis should be on finding a context for the Irish woman poet in that literature. But it is not. Even the

1. An earlier form of this essay appeared in *Creativity and Its Contexts,* ed. Chris Morash (Dublin: Lilliput Press, 1995), 31–47.

words *finding a context* are, I feel, misleading. They imply permissions and al-
lowances—a series of subtle adjustments made to fit a new arrival into an es-
tablished order. I want to make it clear from the start that this is not my view.
It seems to me critical to any accurate or useful interpretation of this subject—
which remains a difficult and controversial one—to insist on this point. I want
to make it very clear from the beginning that any relation between the Irish
woman poet and the national literature is a two-way traffic. That in the
process of finding a context in Irish literature through her work, the woman
poet also redefines the part of that literature which she enacts: namely, Irish
poetry. She also redefines the relation between the national ethos and the Irish
poem. I am not, in other words, talking about some grace-and-favor adjust-
ment of Irish poetry to allow for the new energies of Irish women poets. I
honestly think this is a doomed approach. I am talking about taking this
chance—of new work and radical departures—to look again at Irish poetry
and revise certain assumptions about it.

In his "Modern Poetry: A Broadcast," Yeats makes a striking comment on
T. S. Eliot. "In the third year of the War," he says, "came the most revolu-
tionary man in poetry during my lifetime, though his revolution was stylistic
alone—T. S. Eliot published his first book" ([1936] 1968, 499). It is of
course possible to read this assertion—that Eliot was a radical stylist but little
more—as a conservative, not to say grudging, retrospect. I think a better way
to read it reveals the opposite: that it is, essentially, the rebuke of one great
modernist to another—a rebuke which suggested that Yeats felt Eliot had in-
terpreted the letter of modernism, but may have imperfectly developed its rig-
orous and rewarding spirit. It also—and this is what concerns me
here—contains the implicit warning that changes to poetic form need to hap-
pen at levels deeper than language, mannerism, or influence; that they must
go well beyond those gestures of expression which seem to promise a tempo-
rary shift of fashion or response.

To sustain my view that women poets are influencing the form they enact,
I want to propose a substantive argument for it—one that goes beyond
changes in style or taste. Put as simply as possible, my argument is that both
the Irish poem and the perception of it are radically changed by the fact that
Irish women—within the space of a couple of decades—have gone from being
the objects of the Irish poem to being the authors of it. This does not just
mean that Irish women now write the Irish poem—although they do; it means
they also claim it. Not as their own, I should quickly add: a claim of ownership

should not and cannot be sustained in any art form. Claims of ownership are, in many ways, what women poets have implicitly contested by writing the Irish poem. Nevertheless, they do something exciting and unusual with that poem. Inasmuch as they are the old silent objects of it, now transformed into speaking parts and articulate visions, they make a momentous and instructive transformation in Irish poetry.

And, of course, a contentious one. By enacting their experience and expression within that poem, they have disturbed certain traditional balances in the Irish poem, between object and author, between poet and perspective. These balances were themselves an index and register of an old relation between the Irish poem and the national tradition. Perhaps, at this point, I should change the "they" here to "we." In disrupting such balances, Irish women poets such as myself and Nuala Ní Dhomhnaill and Medbh McGuckian and Paula Meehan have disordered an old, entrenched and even dangerous relation between Irish national assumptions and the Irish poem. Therefore, although I won't say that Irish poetry is at a crossroads, I will say that I believe it has changed. The landscape of it will never be politicized in exactly the same way again. The features of it will never be susceptible to the same definitions again. And the old critiques will not serve anymore in the new situation.

It is always tempting—to choose Yeats's word again—to claim a revolution for the work of any poetic generation. But it is rarely true. And in this case, also, I think there are precedents for the way Irish women poets and Irish poetry connect. I think the mode of connection—the relation of a disruptive energy to a national literature—goes back further than this moment in which poetry by Irish women has become a presence. I think of Irish women poets as refusing the passivity offered them by the inscriptions of a national literature. Their refusal makes a crucial difference and occurs in a crucial area; and I will return to be as precise as I can about it. But in my time, as a young poet in Dublin, I saw and was moved—and I think was also influenced—by the way in which other poets refused different but similar simplifications. I am especially thinking of Patrick Kavanagh. As a poet—like so many of my generation—I continue to find him a liberating force and a poignant, living presence. I am still struck by the way he threw aside shibboleths and symmetries which it might have been thought he would live into, or at least write into. He resisted stereotypes, albeit with pain; he redefined his own power, albeit at cost. Whenever I want to measure that rare and elusive quality which is imaginative courage, I think first of him.

These are affinities and influences, however, they are not critical models. I think it is important to highlight that there is no preexisting critique for the particular conjunction I am speaking about: the emergence of a woman poet against a backdrop of a strong and entrenched national tradition. There are poets, such as Anna Akhmatova, in Russia who were luminously aware, largely through their own experience of it, of the encroachments of power. There are poets like Emily Dickinson, who defined, in her writing, an important puritan ethos, even while she was being eclipsed by it. There are writers like the African-American poet Gwendolyn Brooks who lived at the intersection of race and expression. She speaks for many of the others with her words: "I have heard in the voices of the wind my dim / killed children" (1963, 4).

Nevertheless, the Irish situation is different. It requires a radical and thoughtful approach. It has been, in some senses, stressful for women poets such as myself to have to make the critique, at the same time as we are making the work for which the critique is fitted. I'm afraid it is a measure of the inter-mittent nature of scholarly discussion throughout the seventies and eighties— and what I feel has been a signal failure of the scholarly conferences in this regard—that there has been, until recently, no searching and eloquent critical literature to cover this subject, although there is almost an embarrassment of it in other areas of contemporary Irish poetry. This in turn reflects the as-sumptions—barely stated but easily sensed by a poet like myself—that, while women poets might contribute individual poems, they were unlikely to shift or radicalize the course of Irish poetry itself. I believe there cannot be a sound critique which does not recognize the possibility of their doing so. No poetic tradition is a static or closed entity; it lives to be refreshed and restated, to be strengthened by subversion. In the absence of such a critique, an analysis of the position of the woman poet in the national tradition and literature has only been brought forward through personal witness and private argument. I intend to continue this here.

2

"Poetry," said Rilke, "is the past that breaks out in our hearts." The relation between Irish poetry and the Irish past has always been a subtle and uneasy one. The writer Francis Stuart made a distinction in a letter to the *Irish Times* many years ago. It was a distinction between the state and the nation. The state, he argued—I'm paraphrasing him here from memory—is an expedient construct. It is made of all the downright, day-to-day compromises which everyone perceives as necessary and no one feels bound to. The nation is something different. It is—I am continuing to paraphrase his argument—both more fragile and more communicable: composed of the invisible and the irreducible, and independent of the expedient. Every Irish person has been touched by that nation. Whether they live in Ireland or outside it, anyone who is Irish has encountered it. Whether it emerges for them in songs and stories in childhood, or in reading at a later time, they are aware of it. How they are aware of it is a different matter. There are those who adhere to its visible history; there are those who manipulate it; there are those who are imposed on by it. And there are those—and I include myself—whose first contact with it was through its ambiguities.

The Dublin I began to write in was the Dublin of the early sixties, whereas the Dublin Patrick Kavanagh came to from Monaghan was the Dublin of the late thirties. Vast changes separated those cities: of outlook and custom and politic. Yet both of them—in the narrowly literary sense—were alike in one sense: they remained influenced by the conjunction of the national ethos and Irish poetry. It was not a fortunate conjunction. Kavanagh makes this bitter comment about it in his *Self-Portrait*. "When I came to Dublin," he wrote there, "the Irish Literary Affair was still booming. It was the notion that Dublin was a literary metropolis and Ireland, as invented and patented by Yeats, Lady Gregory and Synge, a spiritual entity. It was full of writers and poets and I am afraid I thought their work had the Irish quality" (1964, 11).

"The Irish quality": Kavanagh's acid reference to it is revealing. It suggests the tension between the private intelligence of the poet and the painfully limiting role he or she may be offered by a national literature. In the objective sense Kavanagh was grappling with something which I would see differently in another generation. The mediation which the Celtic Twilight performed—a mediation of national energies into the Irish poem—had severe consequences for Irish poetry. To start with, Irish nationalism, as it seeped through the rhetoric of the Celtic Twilight, had a heavy and corrupt investment in a false pastoral. Poets like Kavanagh were intended to exemplify the oppressions of Irish history by being oppressed. Kavanagh resisted. He rejected a public role in favor of a private vision. It was a costly and valuable resistance—exemplary to poets like myself who have come later, and with different purposes, into the tradition. I can still be heartened by his defiance of the aftermath of the Twilight—clearly audible in a remark like this, which is also from *Self-Por-*

trait: "In those days in Dublin," he wrote, "the big thing besides being Irish was peasant quality. They were all trying to be peasants. They had been at it for years but I hadn't heard" (1964, 20).

Kavanagh's downright critique of the expectations placed on an Irish poet—albeit in another time—illuminates an aspect of the relation between the Irish poem and the Irish national literature. It also demonstrates that these tensions predate women and their poetry in Ireland, and so may occur whenever a new energy menaces the old configuration of Irish literature.

Heartened by this, I also have a critique to offer. To start with, I challenge certain traditional assumptions about Irish poetry. To say that Irish poetry has taken place against the backdrop of Irish history, which of course it has, is not the same thing as saying that the Irish national ethos has been good for the Irish poem. The two things should not be confused. Irish history is a given; we are all constructed by that construct. The Irish national idea, on the other hand, has always been involved in an ambitious series of propositions. These may have been valuable as articles of faith; they have no value at all as an aesthetic. In putting together the argument of the way in which the Irish woman poet finds a context in a national literature, I am unapologetic about saying that one of the real values—although an extrapoetic one—of women's poetry in this culture is that it shows up the flaws of the relation between Irish poetry and the national ethos. It opens a window on those silences, those false pastorals, those ornamental reductions which a national idea prepares for any literature it hopes will do its work of simplification.

In one important area, where the land and the nation and the feminine figure all come together, the national ethos has instructed the Irish poem in stylization, which has held it back and restricted its idiom. It is important to emphasize that these stresses have not been created by the work of women poets; they have been revealed by them. The best Irish poets have been aware of the dangers of the national tradition; the best work of Irish male poets has always been private, obsessive, and powerful. But there remains in Irish poetry written by men—both in contemporary poetry and the poetry of the past—an available and availed-of image. If I call it Cathleen Ní Houlihan or Dark Rosaleen, I am only giving it disreputable names from another time. But the fusion of the national and the feminine—the old corrupt and corrupting transaction between Irish nationalism and the Irish poem—continues to leave its mark. It is this which the poems of women and by women have disrupted; it is this which their poems have subverted. Irish women poets can therefore be seen as the scripted, subservient emblems of an old image file come to life. In a real sense, the Irish woman poet now is an actual trope who has walked inconveniently out of the text of an ambitious and pervasive national tradition, which found its way into far too much Irish poetry. Her relation to the poetic tradition is defined by the fact that she was once a passive and controlled image within it; her disruption of that control in turn redefines the connection between the Irish poem and the national tradition. And for all these reasons I value the disaffected intelligence of a poet like Louis MacNeice who wrote in "Autumn Journal":

> The land of scholars and saints:
> Scholars and saints my eye, the land of ambush,
> Purblind manifestos, never-ending complaints;
> The born martyr and the gallant ninny;
> The grocer drunk with the drum,
> The landowner shot in his bed, the angry voices
> Piercing the broken fanlight in the slum,
> The shawled woman weeping at the garish altar.
> Kathleen ni Houlihan! Why
> Must a country like a ship or a car, be always female,
> Mother or sweetheart?
>
> (1949, 153)

It stands to reason that poets like Kavanagh and MacNeice, given their time and formation, did not anticipate the role of women poets in Irish poetry. But they addressed tensions which are held in common. Their voices have been a source of information and sustenance in the sometimes difficult task of tracking down those tensions and isolating their effect in Irish poetry. That search has had personal aspects and I think it is pertinent to my argument to speak about those now.

3

I grew up largely outside Ireland. I left at five and returned at fourteen. More importantly, I grew up in a diplomat's house where Ireland was the fictive construct around which our daily life was arranged. My father represented Ireland in Britain. Before that, he had been part of the negotiation by which

Ireland's transition to the status of Republic in the later forties had come about. Ironically, the success of those negotiations, and the achievement of the Republic on foot of them, guaranteed my absence from it.

The outcome of all this was geographically simple and imaginatively complex: I grew up outside Ireland; and I had a nation long before I had a country. It came to me through snatches of conversation, through the unspoken absences of landscape and accents, and through the sentimentalizations which all absences encourage. I listened carefully to the songs and stories, most of which were thrilling and puzzling at the same time. At night I could hear Tom Moore's melodies being played; I could read Mangan's "Dark Rosaleen." A little later, when I was a teenager, I heard Yeats's *Cathleen ni Houlihan* recited on record. It is easy to say now that these were flawed images. The fact is, they were filtered through absence and nostalgia; they stood in as sign for something. That something may have been nothing more—as can be the case with exile—than my own distance from the ambiguities they disguised.

It might have remained like that except that I left school, went to college, and began to publish poetry. I don't think I was particularly skeptical about the nation at that point. I had grown up outside Ireland; I had heard all the songs, the ballads, the formulae of an oppressed entity which are so powerful and so appealing. Which are beyond intelligence; beyond resistance. The first poem I published was called "A Cynic at Kilmainham Gaol." I had no special insight into the flawed connection between a nation and its images. My skepticism, when it came, was not about the nation. It was about the Irish poem.

Is there such a thing as an Irish poem? The question remains a very open one. But there is in any poem, when you disassemble it to look at it more closely, a series of tensions and oppositions which you can see clearly once you look. There is, for instance, in every poem, in every language, the poet's experience and the poet's expression of it. The poet's experience can be of love, or sexuality, of remembrance or disappointment or regional affection. The poet's expression of it is another matter. It is the expression of it, with all its complexities of language and inheritance, that is likely to be instructed, or obstructed, by elements other than private human experience. By nationality, or ideology or polemic. I became powerfully aware in the Dublin of the sixties, although I had no words for it at that stage, that certain elements of experience were, or had been, obstructed by certain elements of expression.

Later I would connect that intuition with the fact that Irish poetry of the forties and fifties—and this was still visible in the sixties—was emerging from a bruising struggle with the aftermath of Yeats. Similarly, Irish poets were emerging from the unnerving relation which the Celtic Twilight has established between the so-called Irish experience and the Irish poem.

Inescapably, Yeats is at the center of this. No other poet will ever mean so much to me as him, and yet he is open to criticism on this account. To go back to that important question—is there such a thing as the Irish poem?—it is clear Yeats thought there was. But the poem he handed on was nevertheless a poisoned chalice for the generation after him. As a construct, it had been supremely useful to Yeats, who knew how to make the Irish cadence, and the Agonistes stance, disrupt the English tradition. But for the poets who followed him, the poem they inherited as a model was an out-of-focus snapshot. By example and insistence, Yeats communicated a poem which was stranded somewhere between British Victorianism and Irish invention. At its worst, it was the poem of what Samuel Beckett called, with wonderful precision, "The Victorian Gael." If, like Yeats, you were the foreground of that poem—an angry, eloquent, and isolated close-up—then what was in the background did not matter so much. If, like Fallon, Clarke, and Kavanagh, you were lost figures in the unfocused background—where the faint shapes of beasts and trees and people happened in a simplified history—then your task was daunting.

These poets had to take that poem, used with such brilliance by a great poet—but inhospitable to their dignity, their identity, their Irish past—and rework it. They had to write a whole psychic terrain back into it, an act made more difficult in that Yeats had blurred that terrain with the power and enticement of simplification. They had to resist those simplifications and restore that complexity. Certainly we have cherished them in our way. But I am not sure we have given them credit for the huge task they faced, the magnetic field they worked in, their stubborn courage. They are the ones who picked up the fragments of a broken mirror and magically repaired them so that we saw ourselves whole. To paraphrase Eliot, if we know more than them, it is because they are what we know.

By now, in a later generation of Irish poetry, I think we've accepted the fact that the Celtic Revival was a powerful, exclusive, and necessary strategy, heavily invested in the passivity of certain images. These images constituted the elements of a false Irish pastoral. That pastoral in turn was necessary to supply the Celtic Twilight with its subtext that Irish culture was somehow both violated and inviolate. The dark side of all this was that Irish poets after Yeats were regularly screen-tested for their supporting roles in this pastoral. It's this in particular, as I've already said, that led Patrick Kavanagh to be so articulate and rhetorical and bitter.

Kavanagh's anger hints at something which the Irish poets of his generation had to deal with. A complex series of evaluations and devaluations; a fragile and dangerous spiral by which their worth—put under stress once by British colonialism—was again called into question, and this time more poignantly and ambiguously, by the towering achievement of a poet with a selective and reactive view of the Irish experience. The origin which inspired them was also the source which menaced them. I take nothing away from Yeats when I argue—as many others have—that he widened and deepened his theme of private humiliation by fueling his argument of a public siege mentality. The dual heritage he left behind was one of the absolute power and redemption of the private theme, and the exclusive and self-deceiving elements of the public one.

The Celtic Twilight therefore had mediated a national tradition into a position of commanding influence on the Irish poem. When I began to write and publish poems in the Dublin of that era, I gradually became aware—once again it was a slow and intuitive process—that although the Celtic Twilight itself was over, there remained a series of subtle, negative permissions surrounding the Irish poem and Irish poetry. The series of evaluations and the devaluations remained. In my case they were held in place, not by a false pastoral—that had gone forever with Kavanagh—but by the intertwining of the feminine and the national.

The poem I inherited contained passive, ornamental images of women. This was particularly true where the woman in the Irish poem in any way suggested the generic, the national, the muse figure. The result of this was not aesthetic; it was highly practical. I took away with me from Dublin, and from Trinity College, a certain kind of Irish poem which was recommended and visible and considered suitable. The national ethos, as it had been allowed into Irish writing, continued to issue certain permissions as to what the poem could be about. You could have a political murder in it, but not a baby. You could have the Dublin hills, but not the suburbs under them. This is a vital point in considering the poem written by the Irish woman poet. The life of the Irish woman—the ordinary, lived life—was invisible and, when it became visible, was considered inappropriate as a theme for Irish poetry. A language of criticism grew up about this. Certain poems were deemed to be "by women" and "for women." The assumptions implicit in that language were that women wrote poems for the constituency of women, and about it. But that these poems were not to be considered binding upon, or subversive of, the mainstream of Irish poetry.

The challenges for women poets in the middle of all this were, and are, many. On the one hand, they could disrupt the permissions issued by the tradition of Irish poetry and put their lives—their gardens, their friendships, their washing machines, their vision of the connection between their life and its expression—into the Irish poem. They have done this; they continue to do it. Women poets in this country whose work I admire and value, such as Paula Meehan and Eiléan Ní Chuilleanáin and Nuala Ní Dhomhnaill and Medbh McGuckian—and there are others—are doing this. When Paula Meehan writes about her mother in "Versions" or Medbh McGuckian canvasses the theme of dislocation in "The Flitting," they are primarily writing good poems. Those poems will be read and valued in places where there is no knowledge of the disruption they caused, the balances they upset, the traditional silences they broke. But the fact that they did all this adds power and poignance to the context. And a generous restructuring of context is at the heart of some of the points I have proposed here.

4

Every new generation of poets, every new departure in poetry—and Irish women poets at the moment constitute both—dramatizes the fact that a poem is assembled in several ways. What I have described here is a personal perspective on some of the tensions in the Irish poem. Of course, the perspective through which an experience is mediated in any poem is, at least partly, the one of the human being who is writing that poem. They are looking back, or looking in, or looking down. They are writing out of love or obsession or hate or emotion and tranquillity, or whatever you like. The part of the poet which is still bound by the experience can be fresh and engaged and innocent of any intervention by ideology or prejudice. But the expressive intelligence of that poet—which can be quite different—is open to many influences.

It has seemed to me that the expressive intelligence of many Irish male poets writing about women—and very much where the image of women inflected the image of the nation—was instructed by the national ethos in a limiting way. This expressive intelligence often obstructed the experience in the poem and turned the woman as subject into the image as object. I have chosen not to go into all the examples in which I see this in the work of male poets of this century in Ireland. Those examples are controversial, and what one person sees another can discount. But I am quite certain that the compound effect of those instructed intelligences was to make the Irish poem unavailable to the ordinary downright and lived experience of women. The result was that the confidence and access of Irish women poets was very much affected by the fact that many of the feminine images in the poetry they inherited partook of the larger confusion between the national and the feminine. For a very long time—in our ballads, our *aisling*[2] poems of the eighteenth century, our nine-teenth-century patriotic verse up to and past Yeats—the feminine drew au-thority from the national in an Irish poem, and the national was softened and disguised through the feminine. I can't think of anything more disruptive than that Irish women poets within a generation should alter that arrange-ment and break the terms of that long-standing contract.

The Irish poem, as it now exists, is a changing interior space. It no longer has predictable component parts. Above all, the historic transaction between the passive/feminine/national and the active/expressive/male Irish poet has been altered. I don't think it will be reestablished. Because of that shift I think we can see more clearly how profoundly nationalism—with all its colors and shadows—is invested in passive feminine images within the Irish poem. Therefore a whole foundation has been undermined, a whole edifice has been and can be cracked, because this shift has happened. With the right openness, the right approach, there is now a chance to look at the past and present of Irish poetry in a fresh and vital way.

Much of this has come about without the help of a preexisting critique. In fact, with rare exceptions, there has been almost the opposite over the last decade. There came to be an unspoken perception that the poem written by a woman might not exactly be an Irish poem. I was often aware, and often con-tested, a damaging suggestion in the air that Irish poetry was one thing—with a clear line of succession and a recognizable assembly of theme—whereas poems by Irish women were something different. Maybe to be accepted; maybe to be valued. But not really to be taken as Irish poems.

What I have said must make it obvious that I challenge this idea. I think it is damaging in equal proportions to poetry written by women and to Irish lit-

2. Dream or vision.

erature. The poetry being written by women in Ireland today is Irish poetry. It stands in the mainstream of that valuable tradition; and like all such entries into a tradition, it reorders what is there.

When I was a young poet the restrictions and flawed permissions of the poem I inherited, and the climate I wrote in, were acute enough that it seemed I would be faced by an ethical choice I could not make and would not want: that I could only be the woman poet I wished to be if I turned my back on the power and enrichment of the national tradition. Or that I could be an Irish poet, but only at the cost of exploring my identity as a woman poet. At that point it seemed that my Irishness and my womanhood were on a collision course in my poetry.

It did not happen. The choice was illusory. But it intensified my commitment to see in Irish poetry a diverse and challenging critique. Which will allow for new energies and stem tests. Which will not marginalize the awkward and subversive. Which makes generous gestures to the new and disruptive. I do not know how this is going to happen if there is not a new way of thinking to go with a new way of writing the Irish poem.

I want to be as candid at the end as I was at the beginning. I believe there has been real resistance to the views I propose here among the community of scholars who write about Irish poetry. The connection between Irish women poets and that community has not been, in my view, especially useful or illuminating. There are, of course, sustaining exceptions. But by and large there has been a scholarly tendency to consider poetry by Irish women poets as an inscription on the margin of Irish poetry. I do not hold this view. I do not think it is an accurate view. I do not think it serves Irish poetry well. I think it is partially responsible for the mistaken exclusions— and subsequent distortions—in the recent *Field Day Anthology of Irish Writing* (1991).

Because of the rearrangements and the innovations of the recent past, a woman in Ireland who wishes to inscribe her life in a poem has a better chance now to move freely around within that poem, to select its subject and object at will, and to redirect its themes to her purposes. I would be deeply disappointed if this were construed, at this late stage, by the scholarly community as merely an advantage to women poets in Ireland. It constitutes an increase in artistic freedom, a precious addition of idiom and vista in what is already one of our most precious possessions: the Irish poem.

Joan Newmann. Photograph by Kate Newmann.

Joan Newmann

Apple

For Ailbhe

Which apple?
Lord Lambourne? Worcester Permain?
Woody bitter crab?
Apples of childhood without names?
Yellow-skinned, vaguely musty,
A neighbor's gift, windfalls,
Brown splotch of decay.

Apples on the Old Rectory trees,
Sitting, summer legs, sore on branches,
Eating at autumn with the reach of a hand,
Throwing sucked cores down through golden air
For fussy russet hens to run at.

Loughgall and Richill Bramleys,
Peeled in a white delph bowl, turning tan:
Shush of knife on apple flesh.
Stolen slices, sugar crystals moist
On moisture—tart, tart.

The apple, green as green Granny Smith
Eileen McKenna and I bought

In Cissie White's for ninepence.
Her, walking me part of the way home,
Passing it for jaw-sized bites,
Slobbering juices on our chins.
Perfection. Past our bedtime and it still light.

Adam, I did not give you the apple.
Had you not taken, bitten strong,
Colour for the hungry soul,
Essence skiting from your teeth,
We never would have known.

Coming of Age

The child you are is part of the woman you will become. It was the War. I was born in August 1942. American soldiers were billeted in Tandragee Castle. They gave us gifts of chocolate and chewing gum. We were a matriarchy, my aunts, my mother, and myself. There was lightness and laughter.

In 1945 the men came home, but not my father, whom I did not know, and we had to adjust. A listening child—"She could hear the grass grow"—a remembering child. My uncle made me a wooden horse, Dobbin, the rhythm of the rockers and the rhythm of rhymes.

I am sitting on the floor between the open doors of a sideboard and I have levered the lid from a tin of dried eggs with a spoon. I have spooned a dessert spoon of what looks like custard powder into my mouth and it is swelling the full of it, with my saliva. I can neither swallow it nor spit it out. I sit, guilty.

Maggie Joyce and Fred, visiting on Sunday evening—the colorful, energetic talk, the naming of people—the lure of gossip—and late supper with sandwiches and home-baked cake.

I am taken to Gertie Abraham the dressmaker's on the carrier of my aunt's bicycle. The smells of growing and cattle and people's gardens, and the man who keeps peacocks, and the breathless rush of air.

Oh, the great days before school, all things possible. You could tell yourself anything you wanted. A precious time before teachers who didn't like people—the other pupils—whose own distinct and very different living you could sense. It was all the lowest common denominator. A savage tonsillectomy with a soap and water enema—the little boy in the ward who screamed when the curtains were drawn—the awful, secret thing wrong with him (in time I knew—a circumcision).

I am at Muriel's. It is too soon after hospital. They give me milky tea. It goes up the back of my nose where my tonsils and adenoids used to be. It shoots in two powerful jets down my nostrils—all over my new, duck-egg blue woolen dress. When I tell her, my mother thinks I am lying, though she doesn't say anything. I try to describe the suddenness of it—the mess of it—searching to find the words for the shock of it. I want her to know. She says, "It's all right."

I was unready for school. I could read and write with ease, and it must have been a visit from the school attendance officer that brought a hush on the house.

Mrs. Greenlee, who used to stand behind you and thump you between the shoulder blades if you copied a letter down wrongly from the blackboard. This wasn't learning, and I had never been so uncomfortably close to other people's unhappiness, snot, and tears. Mrs. Greenlee had cancer. Though a dead badger or fox on the road stilled my breath, I had difficulty mourning her.

Miss Robb didn't see that big Betty Webb was nipping me hard under the desk. When I pointed it out, I was moved as if I were the troublemaker. Injustice, and it all a terrible waste of time. The next year was little better: Mrs. Marshall, the wife of the headmaster. I was learning to hood my watchfulness—to only half-listen—to attempt to speak in received pronunciation. Mrs. Marshall was keen on elocution. The richness of our County Armagh accent (people said "tay" instead of "tea," and "wine" instead of "wind"—Elizabethan English, Armagh having been settled in the Plantation by people from Stratford-on-Avon). I went home, accentuating my "ings" to find a smirk appear on the kindest faces. On my first trip to London the people there could not understand a word I said.

We are in the front room. It has snowed all day—caked high along the windowsill. My aunts are going to a parish social. Carrie is putting men's hand-knit woolen socks, the color of moss, over her shoes. My mother and I wait in the firelight, the coal turning to red cinder—listening. Gert comes back saying that Carrie has fallen into a snowdrift. That she can't get up. "She says she heard her bone crack, in her leg. . . . No. I don't think it's through the skin, but I can't see. Joe Quinn has phoned for the ambulance." She leaves. I want to go. My mother says there is nothing we can do. I know that there is. There is. The light in the room is not light enough.

Mr. Marshall, calling us in from the snow.

"Go home and tell your Da, then," somebody shouted at Betty Pedlow.

"It's more than Joan Watton can do anyway," she yelled back into frosty air.

"Betty Pedlow insulted me, sir."

Our frozen hands outstretched for the cane. A furrow becoming a weal on not one but both my hands.

I am going to Betsy Irwin's. On the road a small, hurt bird, flapping and afraid. I make a pocket for him by folding up my skirt. We build a nest in the old pump where the cats can't get him till he is well. I know that today he will be ready to fly. "Sammy filled the pump with water. The bird got drowned." I am enraged. Betsy says her mother says I am not to go back. I say I wouldn't anyway.

And there was Sunday School—a dreary time—and church, saved only by some hymns and odd words: "left undone those things that we ought to have done and we have done those things that we ought not to have done," that and "peace which passeth all understanding." I had a good, expensive coat and shoes, that wretched churchy thing of being seen to be well dressed. The mile walk in all weathers. Gwen and Betty Milligan telling me that a seam opened in your belly and babies came out.

I was an anomalous creature, going to school in a different parish: I was on the outside. I remember being told by a stranger not to suck the elastic band under my chin which kept my hat on.

Brethren Sunday School in the afternoons because Willie Thornton, who ran it, was my mother's cousin. I would wait outside our house for their car, learning verses from the Bible. If you got it right, you got a bar of chocolate. The Bible was full of the most amazing, furtive information: Onan who spilled his seed on the ground I didn't understand for a long time; Jacob and the con-cubines, and Reuben and Joseph being only half-brothers.

Clean hands or dirty hands,
Brown eyes or blue,
Pale cheeks or rosy cheeks,
Jesus loves you.
Come to Him while you may,
He will wash your sins away.
Clean hands or dirty hands,
Brown eyes or blue.

Being reborn remains a mystery to me.

This juxtaposed at home with:
Poyntzpass, kiss my ass,
Tandragee and Scarva.
And
Some say the divil's dead,
Some say he's hardly,
Some say he's up in bed,
Fiddling with his charlie.
And
Mary, Mary had a canary,
Up the leg of her drawers.
These—my poetic traditions.

Mrs. Caughey was my salvation at primary school. She played the piano and taught us rare and beautiful folk songs—some of which I have never heard since:
The dress that she wore was a velvet so green,
All trimmed with gold lace and bright as the sea.

Mrs. Caughey, her laugh like a gentle arpeggio, her grey hair drawn back in a bun, her neat pink blouses, white blouses, blue blouses under her navy blue suit. I won her heart when I brought half the contents of our house into school for the staging of *Alice in Wonderland* and I was a wondrous dormouse. I think Hilary Magennis got sick and that on the night I was Alice. I might only have wished this. "Write your own last verse for homework," she'd say, after we had learned a song—and I could. I could do it very well. I could do it better than anybody else.

In secondary school I hear she is dying of cancer. I gather the full of my hands of primroses—a huge circle of pale yellow heads, female bearing the brown seed, male the green pistil, wrapped in grease-proof paper, tied to the carrier of my bike. Her hair cropped, her beautiful face distended with drugs and suffering lowered itself to the incomparable scent, and I slowly realized that she, my teacher, was crying—crying, in front of me.

There was the bike, got at last on hire purchase and too late. An ugly thing to the eye—maroon and curved where it should have been straight. Pam Quinn's was angular and shining pale blue with gears. And when I was ten my mother, who was forty-eight, got a very severe stroke, which affected her speech. She was paralyzed down her right side and had to be dressed and taken to the toilet, tasks I sometimes undertook with zeal. Home was, as Emily Dickinson says, where the house was.

I am in the shed where my uncle does his carpentry—the magical green gulp of the spirit level—how to set the teeth of a saw—dove-tailing—heavy jam pots of nails poured and put in sizes—fed up, mixed up—put back in, clinking, smell of metal on fingers. The song of the plane—sometimes sticking on knots—resuming. I lock him in one day—forget. It is Saturday. He misses football. He falls out with me.

I am making hay at Muriel Cullen's—the turning and the shaking—the sun high—the hayseed itch in the clothes, the hair. Standing—tramping the stack—higher and higher. If you got giddy and slid off, bringing a drift of hay in both hands, the men got cross. It was work. The rope made with the twisting of hay—Muriel's granda—the throwing it over to hold in the wind—and another one. And we were sent to the house to help carry the tea—big milky pots of it and warm soda bread and homemade butter with ribs and a thistle on it—maybe rhubarb jam. Hay seeds in my ears and the best of sleep.

A country child, even if a mainish road from Portadown to Newry ran above our house on its acre of ground. Laborers' Cottages they were called when they were built at the turn of the century, but there was little land laboring now and most families had at least one person working in a factory. Carrie got up each day at seven—came home at six—her dinner kept in the oven: potatoes, cabbage, bacon. I remember. She would slip me a forkful—my mouth open at the scandal brought home and the wholeness of us all—a callous on her finger from weaving and holding scissors to cut the linen yarn; a gentle settle of factory dust on her black cardigan, on her eyebrows; oh, the talking and the listening the whole of the evening. The love in her.

At school I get chicken pox: calamine lotion, calamine lotion. "If you pick the spots you'll be scarred for life." And mumps: I need fish. White fish. It is Friday. My aunt Gert cycles to Tandragee. While it's cooking, its awful smell inhabits me. I cannot even look at it. And measles.

I listen to the radio. I take into myself anything it can give me. Those great three-hour-long plays on Saturday and Sunday evenings, "The Bride of Lammermoor," it getting dark, the fire going out—afraid to move.

I knew the best places for blackberries and frogspawn—the bank in Quinn's field with a billion primroses—where the bluebells grew and the wild strawberries and what mushrooms were edible. I had a place, the corner of Sam Irwin's field with mossy stones, a stream loud enough to gurgle like running water, where violets and ferns grew, and where I couldn't be seen from the road. Lime green light, not just late evening sun, shining only on me.

I am traveling in Joe Quinn's car to Warrenpoint. Pam is there, but between us sits Shirley, as delicate as a pale freesia. She has had her appendix taken out. Each time we pass over a bump on the road we hear her intake of breath. Her father looks anxiously in the rearview mirror. She is wearing a pale dress with all the flowers of summer shadowed on it. Her feet are thin, thin. And her wrists. I breathe away from her, pressing myself tight against the door of the car. If I lurch towards her, Shirley Quinn will break.

Secondary school. No Irish history—only what happened in other places. Secondary school, delicate business of making friends, the boys, listening to Radio Luxembourg for the top twenty, my claiming life. Shadowed by my mother's death when I was fourteen. The monstrous heat before a storm, the smell of lavender water, my mother in white satin tinged with mauve in lightning, in her room. The demented group of us under the sycamore tree watching the funeral leave us. Setting the table for one too many. The confusion, the dislocation of everything I had learned. Shouting at a teacher who was chiding me for doing poorly in a test: "Your mother didn't die during the summer holidays!" and how strange and macabre it sounded in the air. All that, and the fact that my father might claim me.

The anchors. A supply teacher for whom I wrote about my London trip—my Uncle Bill had taken me to the East End on the Woolwich ferry and had warned me that I wouldn't see Sunday School sights—pages, oh pages of it. "It's an extraordinary piece of work. I gave it to my husband to read and he says have you thought of a career as a journalist." No.

I am climbing Slieve Donard with John Scott. All the girls love John Scott. Only to breathe the same air. Cloud comes down on us and a mountain wet. I sit next to John Scott shivering and smiling on the mountaintop. One thousand seven hundred and sixty-five feet. How was it that in the end I was thigh to thigh with Percy Patterson, his arm too tight around my waist because he couldn't see with the rain on his glasses?

There were Miss Gilchrist and Miss Lynas, two truly remarkable teachers—reading D. H. Lawrence's "Snake" and T. S. Eliot's "Journey of the Magi" from what was a fairly tawdry anthology. I loved the words. The words, the sounds, the play on the senses, the visions.

I wrote my first long poem, a terrible thing with which I was wholly involved—a soldier who had deserted, dying in a ditch trying to justify his actions. During the gap between giving this poem to Miss Gilchrist and waiting nervously for its return, I began to doubt its worth. She was kind—what a strange subject for a young girl to choose; full of energy and color; keep writing; it's a great gift.

I loved Miss Lynas but I know she loved the Maths teacher. The day we watched Lawrence Olivier's *Hamlet* she wore the bunch of violets I had spent much time picking for her, on the lapel of her grey wool suit. The darkness, the poetry of Shakespeare, and Miss Lynas with my flowers under the same roof. Oh.

The great gift got siphoned off into school subjects. I took Keats's "Ode to a Nightingale" into myself, and, given the right wine, I can still quote it forty years on.

I wanted to be a teacher. My family didn't say anything. A silence. It would mean a period of training when I might otherwise be earning money. And the disease that was inbuilt in my particular, reticent society—I mightn't be able to do it. A risk. You didn't take risks because that was the way to end up in the gutter. In retrospect, and since I did belatedly become a teacher, it was the gods protecting me. Stewart Parker, the Irish playwright, once said to me that it wasn't possible to teach and write. The teaching took the energy; the writing, if it was given anything at all, got what was left. Examinations; the shaft of lime green light shone only on me.

◁

I worked first in the Bank of Ireland—opening the post, photocopying. It had wonderful marble interior pillars which had been allowed to grow grimy because of an anticipated move to a new building. As high as my arm could reach from chair level, I scrubbed, sat, wearied by the incarceration, surrounded by gloriously shiny Italian marble columns. I found the subservience of the women employees appalling. Many of them had spent their working lives in this vault.

I moved to the Civil Service—Clerical Assistant, and though the hierarchies were constricting, I was so close to the bottom that I was largely ignored. If I organized my work, it could be dispatched within no time. And I wrote more and read more during that period than I have ever been able to since. "Betrayal" came to me, fully formed, after I had spent a lunchtime staring at newts in a tank, melting away the tired office walls and leaving me in that other, precious world.

I am living in a flat in Claremont Street—on the second floor. The chimney is blocked—no fires. In the oven a dehydrated carcass of a chicken left by my predecessor on a roasting tray. A big uncomfortable bed, a gas fire, books on the mantelpiece, and my mother's patchwork quilt. A shared bath—no water from the taps. To Smoky Joe's for rissoles and chips, rissoles and chips, rissoles and chips. Quarter bottles of surreptitious whiskey bought from John Rath. This is living. At the weekend men urinate and swear in the alley under my barred window. And on her landing in her pink candlewick dressing gown and fluffy slippers, Mrs. Sinton, who was bewildered and lonely: "You'll have to come in for a cup of tea someday." I never did.

I had a great office companion, Jimmy McConville. We were good to each other. He sensed when I didn't have any money. Half his lunch, a soda farl and tuna, would appear on my desk. "But sure, I have far too much and I'd rather have the drink than the food." He used to dry out his hanky in front of the stove and say, "You see that steam—that's pure gin."

I could see women around me being kept down—women at home working till it became a fearsome habit which no one remarked on—women who were spirited but who feared men's anger and men's cruelty.

I am joining extramural night classes. Workers' Educational Association night classes. Everything. My night is becoming my day. Philip Hobsbaum is one of my tutors—an inspired and inspiring teacher. "I have these poems . . ." Yes, he'd read them. Nothing all summer. Then a glorious twenty-four pages—a critique of each poem. An invitation to join the Belfast Group to be started in October. Write it all out of me; the now, the wherefore, the silences.

The Group was.

I am knocking on the door of a flat in Fitzwilliam Street—feet on many stairs. At the top of the first flight of stairs, a wonderful smell of curry. More stairs. A large room—three long windows—books, on books, on books, on books. A great coming together.

A quiet man in himself, blonde-haired, smoking a pipe—translating poems from Catalonian. Arthur Terry, Professor of Spanish.

The structure was formal. The Group met once a week.

Watchful as a bird—a justice about him—good stories with desire muted—to become a friend in time. Hugh Bredin.

Each session dealt with the work of an individual which was circulated on broadsheets to all the other members of the Group the previous week, usually six poems or one short story.

As gentle as waves at a lake's edge—her ginger hair masking her face as she read—Marilyn Stronge's boat poem—her liquid voice: "To and fro, to and fro."

Each piece of writing was thoroughly scrutinized, and the criticism was constructive.

Wire-framed glasses—curly hair—Beckettian sense of humor—an artificial leg—the poems, the prose, the song, and eventually the many plays. *I'm a dreamer Montreal.* Saying the amputation—to let him through to saying everything. He's dead, and oh the difference. Stewart Parker.

Philip chaired the meetings, and the ethos he created and sustained was one of pleasure and discovery. There was no space for destruction.

Fierce and involved without malice—poems that grew like unexpected flowers in dry places. Nick Round.

There were certain unspoken rules: you did not come unprepared; you attended regularly, not only when your own work was being discussed; you did not come with drink taken and you were not late.

Passionate stories, long and seeking without consummations—without even the taking off of socks. We were reading *Lady Chatterly's Lover.* Maurice Gallagher.

What united us was what each of us brought to the Group; what you were able to write and a generous intellectual and emotional engagement in the writing of the others.

Tulips on Queen's' lawn—a good poem about a telephone box—a good-looking student finding his own worth. Brian Scott.

It was Philip Hobsbaum's genius and magnanimity which generated the energy, keeping us together.

The devil's advocate—a student—I feared his cutting tongue for the sake of it—John Bond. He hated everything—nearly.

I was asked by a "Group biographer" if we were encouraged to write "Group poetry." No. A wide variety of work was written and read.

Indian and regal and there in her own right. Sure of what she needed to say, needed to write. Hannah Hobsbaum.

Another question which the biographer asked was, Did we know that the Group sheets were being circulated to Philip's friends, mostly members of the London Group (Edward Lucie-Smith, Martin Bell, George MacBeth) to which he had belonged? This was phrased as if it would be a shocking revelation.

Confident, vocal student—enthusiastic participant in discussion, Angela McCourt. She married John Bond.

I feel that there was not one person there who did not completely and unquestioningly trust Philip Hobsbaum with her work.

"I'm not a writer. I'm here to hear." Cosmopolitan. At ease. "It's a pity

Queen's doesn't have a Festival." "Well, start one," Philip said. Michael Emerson did. Philip was keen to help us achieve publication, to fill the university magazine, *Interest*, with our new poetry, and to organize readings, and some people had poems accepted by George MacBeth on BBC Radio 3.

Eager, glad to be there, intelligent. A student. Ian Christie. I see the name in high places.

Philip Hobsbaum has not been given full credit for what he achieved.

Bearded, guitared, with a wonderful singing voice. James Simmons. A teacher, with five children. His lyrics, his poetry—to Nigeria. I live with Laura, Rachel, Sarah, Adam, Helen, and Penelope. They all leave for Nigeria.

Philip was a published poet himself, yet he nurtured the gift of so many others.

Smiling with all of him, discerning, a match for any man, Seamus Heaney. *Death of a Naturalist* (1966) showed us the way—or that we'd lost it.

A Jewish background, so Protestant/Catholic did not spell obstruction to him. Articulate, intense, seeing and aware of the importance of the Group even then. A love of poetry. Philip Hobsbaum.

And there was me.

Certain poets were favored by the Group, Philip Larkin in particular, and I remember the celebration of *Whitsun Weddings* (1964). Donald Hall's *Contemporary American Poetry*, published by Penguin in 1962, was welcomed with great enthusiasm, and Galway Kinnell's extract from "The Avenue Bearing the Initial of Christ into the New World" astounded us all.

Retrospectively, Denise Levertov and Adrienne Rich perhaps did not get as much attention as they deserved.

➣

I am walking in the snow. The telephone lines are down. There is no traffic on the road. I run, sliding on ice, joyful. I walk four miles from Holywood to Belfast—freezing air burning my face. I could trek to the North Pole. A strawberry, cherry, raspberry, apricot sunset, spilling across the horizon. It is the greatest day. I need to tell them I am pregnant.

In 1965 nine pamphlets were published by Festival Publications, Queen's University, Belfast. They cost two shillings and sixpence each or one pound for the series. The poets were Michael Longley, Seamus Heaney, Derek Mahon, Arthur Terry, Joan Newmann, Philip Hobsbaum, Stewart Parker, James Simmons, and Seamus Deane. I undertook to distribute them to American universities. Seamus Heaney refers to them as the Sun Blest pamphlets (Sun Blest bread and the pamphlets had a similar logo). They make extraordinary reading.

I am a poet.

Seamus Heaney has *Death of a Naturalist* (1966) published (and a splendid book it is), and Stewart Parker is beginning to have his plays staged. The poetry I listen to: the songs of Joni Mitchell, John Lennon, Dory Previn, Randy Newman, and the Incredible String Band; and I love the work of Margaret Lawrence, Margaret Atwood, and Alice Munroe.

I meet my father.

> Father you left me but I never left you
> I need you but you didn't need me
> (John Lennon, from "Mother")

Winter fir trees on the curve of the hill—light dying. Nothing. I lie, my face on stones, my lips on stones, trying to tell them my address. Kate will be home from school. Before the ambulance arrives I am put, unconscious, in a military ambulance. The corpse on the stretcher is placed on the floor. The ambulance driver tells me later, "We thought you were a shovel and polythene bag job." He then plays his guitar and sings "Amazing Grace" that strange Sunday. The nurse who keeps me alive in the night whispers that she is going to be married soon. I would like to buy her something extraordinary. The woman who lies opposite me says that the night I arrived they had a beautiful tea, Chicken Maryland and chips, and that the look of me put her off hers. I hear myself apologize.

I limp back.

Coming of Age comes of age in 1995.

Moya Cannon. Photograph by Mike Shaughnessy.

Moya Cannon

Night

Coming back from Cloghane
in the sudden frost
of a November night,
I was ambushed
by the river of stars.

Disarmed by lit skies
I had utterly forgotten
this arc of darkness,
this black night
where the frost-hammered stars
were notes thrown from a chanter,
crans of light.

So I wasn't ready
for the dreadful glamour of Orion
as he struck out over Barr dTrí gCom
in his belt of stars.

At the Gleann na nGealt
his bow of stars
was drawn against my heart.

What could I do?

Rather than drive into a pitch-black ditch
I got out twice,
leaned back against the car
and stared up at our windy, untidy loft
where old people had flung up old junk
they'd thought might come in handy,
ploughs, ladles, bears, lions, a clatter of heroes,
a few heroines, a path for the white cow, a swan
and, low down, almost within reach,
Venus, completely unfazed by the frost.

(Cannon 1997, 40–41)

The Poetry of What Happens

> The things that concern you most can't be put in prose
> —Theodore Roethke (1972, 171)

A few nights ago I was fortunate enough to be present at a particularly enjoyable night of traditional music—special because a certain balance and communication between the musicians and the twenty or twenty-five other people in the room. The listeners were able to give the musicians just enough silence to play an unforced music. The two musicians at the heart of the session were then able, in turn, to create a relaxed atmosphere where it was possible to draw songs from their listeners. It had never struck me so forcibly before that music is largely a function of silence. Only silence can allow music to happen. I wondered then what allows poetry to happen. I think that poetry is in some sense a function of chaos, or at least a function of contradiction. Insofar as poetry happened to me, it happened in the context of trying to make my way out of some sort of chaos.

I first became alerted to poetry at the age of about nineteen. Over the course of a year or two, an older brother lent or gave me presents of a few collections—*The Captain's Verses* by Neruda (1972), a collection by Yevtushenko. An Australian friend kindly sent me a beautiful cloth-bound collection of haiku after I had unkindly kidnapped the volume which she had brought with her to Ireland as holiday reading. I no longer have any of these books but can remember the texture of the paper and the print in each one of them. They were read and reread with an attention given to almost none of the books which I now own. There was a total absorption with each volume in its turn, with no element at all of "comparing and contrasting." In addition to enjoying the poetry as poetry, there was also the breezy exhilaration of a first encounter with the sensibilities of other cultures.

About this time a complimentary reference to Ezra Pound, which I had come upon in my very scanty readings of Joyce, led me to Pound's versions from the Chinese and his later essays. Pound's emphasis on the value of translation, the centrality of cadence, his respect for the song-makers of the romance tradition brought me back to the words of some of the Irish songs which I had come across at school, to Douglas Hyde's *Love Songs of Connacht* ([1904], 1971), to Eilís Dillon's translation of *Caoineadh Art Uí Laoighre* (1980), and to translations of the early Irish nature lyrics. What drew me to these was, firstly, the hammered beauty of their music and imagery and, secondly, the way in which their aesthetic undermined the model of historical progress which I had acquired as a student of history and politics. If relatively uneducated or unlettered country people could, in the eighth or fifteenth or nineteenth century, so skillfully evoke moments of tenderness, or passion, or sheer beauty, if these words were sufficiently valued by their communities to allow of their preservation, then a linear model of human progress, where we had evolved upwardly from ignorance and superstition into the light of reason, was quite inadequate. I found great solace in the felt evidence that humanity was much deeper and richer than such a model could allow.

It was the same sort of solace which I found in certain objects in the National Museum in Dublin, when I used occasionally to wander in on a wet Saturday: the gold lunulae or collars, particularly the simple earlier ones which consisted of a twisted strip of gold; a long dugout canoe, which rested on top of the glass display cases on the left-hand side of the main exhibition area; and a bog oak or bog ash statue of St. Molaoise which came originally, I think, from Inishmurray in County Sligo. This statue was quite unlike anything I had ever seen before. In its composure the figure was much more like an Eastern sage than any saint I had ever come across, and it seemed to pass on some of its composure to my disheveled spirit. All of these objects spoke clearly of the sensibility of those who had made and minded them. The felt evidence of skill, texture and beauty discounted the idea that these people were any less sensitive to their surroundings than the people whom I knew. I had no vocabulary with which to express any of this experience and found it difficult enough to fit into the worldviews to which I had been exposed at that time. It is, of course, impossible at any time to prove that something is beautiful or that beauty has any value at all.

I may be oversimplifying slightly in saying that I had slipped from a passive acceptance of one dogma into a passive acceptance of another—from the conservative Catholicism of rural Ireland to the simplified Marxism of student Dublin in the mid-seventies. Although there was, and is, much which I would value in both traditions, in Marxism, as in the Catholicism which I knew, there were huge areas of experience which were either completely beyond the pale or for which the theory provided no language at all. John Berger put the problem very succinctly in a recent interview: "Marxism—and this is very important—. . . doesn't have of itself an aesthetics, any more than it has an ethics. This is the lacuna in Marxism. There were Marxists who behaved disgustingly, but there were also millions who behaved with incredible self-sacrifice, and with great ethical nobility. But this came from themselves; it didn't come from Marxism" (1996, 36).

There seems to be an urgent need for the assurance of an aesthetic during the late teens and twenties, a need from which the music industry, for instance, has profited greatly. The need is there right through life, but perhaps it is particularly intense at that age. I started to write in my early twenties in an attempt to cope with a great deal of inner confusion. I had left college, found myself in a demanding teaching position, and looked about for some relief. It is common to dismiss much poetry as merely therapeutic. Certainly a great deal of bad poetry is produced whose sole function is to spill out the troubles of the writer. It may be unfortunate that so much of this is printed. Bad poetry of this kind does, however, need to be written. I am reminded of something I heard at about this time in a radio interview with Madge Herron, the Donegal poet. She said, in the context of a question about writers' workshops, "You have to write the bad poetry out of yourself before you can write good poetry." The observation struck me with all the force of an uncomfortable truth. Real poetry was always written under some sort of pressure. Initially, at least, it is important to spit out your bother. What has been spat out should not be mistaken for poetry, yet, in the early stages of writing, we are so relieved to have externalized our turmoil that we often do so. It is generally only the raw material of poetry. But once it has been literally *ex-pressed* and externalized, it is possible to cast about for the images which will make sense of it. It is only through the medium of image and rhythm that communication and consequently poetry is possible. However, without the initial pressure or tension—without, at least, something to wonder about—the most meticulous attention to craft and form will produce no more than an empty crate.

In an essay of this sort which focuses on particular books, particular encounters, which either nourished or provoked, it is easy to overlook or forget to mention a lot of given circumstances or influences. Poetry was an important part of the literature course both in primary and in secondary school, and I was fortunate in having excellent teachers. Also, in my mother's family, as in much of the north of Ireland, the "recitation" had been very much part of any social occasion. Many of these recitations were of the romantic, nationalist school; many were of the local humorous genre and Robbie Burns was a staple. So from an early age it seemed natural enough for me to "learn off" ballads for my own amusement. In Dublin during the late seventies and early eighties, I took part in a most enjoyable and anarchic workshop in the Grapevine Arts Centre. Its instigator was Dermot Bolger, and among the participants were Anne Hartigan, Pat McCabe, Pauline Fayne, and a rather atypical member of the Armed Forces named Donal Dempsey. Donal used to risk life and limb in illicitly copying his poems—by torchlight, if I remember correctly—on the Department of Defense's photocopier. (Photocopies were expensive in the seventies.) Apart from the flashes of literary excellence which make a workshop worthwhile, what I remember most about the Grapevine was the aggregate enthusiasm and humor. I also found it a most useful sounding board in a time when I was fumbling with the acquisition of basic skills. Most of us were fairly innocent of literary theory and could therefore get on with the job of learning how to write. This is not to say that we were free of literary fashion. A friend of mine who used to come along for moral support remarked on the extraordinary frequency with which umbilical cords featured in the poems. Urban angst was also in vogue. This didn't suit me too well, because, although I had no shortage of angst, it remained inconveniently rural.

It is hard to know whether any writer chooses her or his subject or whether the subject does the choosing. Almost from the start the metaphors available to me related to landscape, language, and place-names, that most tangible of etymologies, the interface between language and landscape. I have always wondered how, among all the possible names, one adheres to a place; how such a tacit consensus is arrived at. Some criterion of oppositeness applies which is very similar to that which applies in the writing of poetry—it is the salient description which sticks, as if somehow the land has colluded in writing the poem of itself and the people who lived on it.

I had begun to read a lot more Irish poetry at this time and particularly liked the work of John Montague and Francis Harvey. I was drawn to the lucid imagery and musicality of both poets. Also perhaps, particularly in Harvey's poems, the country people whom he described were people who were utterly familiar to me, the textures and weathers of their lives inseparable from the textures of their lands, the unarticulated tragedies of their lives imploding into the culture into which I had been born. I was perhaps one generation removed from the culture which Harvey described. My parents were the first generation of country people who had had access to more than a primary education. Both of them taught, and both, in different ways, were interested in poetry. My father, who came from an Irish-speaking area in South Donegal, wrote and published poems in Irish under a female Irish *nom de plume,* Róise Nic A'Ghoill. Such a subterfuge would be seen as highly suspect now, but he regarded it as a very clever play on the local place-name *Ros Goill.* He also joked occasionally about a brief, semiflirtatious exchange of letters between Róise and Séan Ó Riordáin, one of the senior figures in Irish-language poetry at the time. My mother, who had been brought up in mid-Tyrone, also spoke Irish but was more interested in English literature, and had been a good friend of the poet Alice Milligan, who, in her later years, lived not far from my mother's home village of Carrickmore. Apart from nursery rhymes, the first poem which I can remember learning was Alice's:

> When I was a little girl
> In a garden playing,
> A thing was often said
> To chide us, delaying:
>
> When after sunny hours,
> At twilight's falling,

Down through the garden walks
Came our old nurse calling—

"Come in! for it's growing late,
And the grass will wet ye!
Come in! or when it's dark
The Fenians will get ye."
(1993, 50)

Born in the late fifties, I was one of the generation brought up and schooled
in the sixties on a heady romantic nationalism, which was to be rapidly dero-
manticized by the realities of the northern troubles. I was also part of the
free education generation. Free secondary education was introduced in
1967, the year before I went to secondary school, and grant-aided third-level
education in 1968. This increased access to education is probably a major
factor both in the general artistic renaissance and in the renaissance in
women's writing which we are currently witnessing in Ireland. Until then
there was probably an element of "the conservative teaching the conserva-
tive" in Irish education. The educational system reinforced the attitude ex-
pressed in the 1937 constitution, that a woman's proper role was that of
nurturer and facilitator.

〜

I began to write at a time when I was very confused. Confused times can be
fertile times for no other reason, perhaps, than that our need to bring order
out of the unbearability of chaos forces us into the difficult business of making
something new, into feeling and thinking our way in new directions and into
certain valuable recognitions which would not previously have been possible.
In an odd way, books, like people, do sometimes cross our paths just when we
need them or can recognize their worth. One such book, in my own case, was
Kathleen Raine's *Defending Ancient Springs* (1967), which I came across
when I had been writing and publishing in journals for a few years. What I
liked in it was Raine's rather unfashionable belief in the existence of an unde-
constructible source for poetry, of the centrality of some sense of the spiritual
at the heart of art and of the role of art in nurturing the human spirit. It ac-
corded with intuitions which I had had about the violence of trying to decon-
struct the core of beauty in, say, the early Irish nature lyrics, in terms of their
historical, sociological, and psychological components. Call it by any other

name, the synthesis of sound and rhythm which could alert or disarm the heart, which could acknowledge depths of passion, moments of candor, was in some sense miraculous.

⁀

Intellectual climates change so rapidly and so drastically that it is sometimes difficult to remember the weather of previous decades. For an Irish student in the seventies to have spoken, or even thought, outside the terms of logical positivism was hardly possible. To admit to a spiritual dimension to human life was to align oneself with the institutions which laid claim to the governance of the nation's spiritual life, the Irish Catholic Church. Since it had chosen to operate also as an institution of secular power, in becoming a *de facto* established church, and had greatly discredited itself in this regard, that vocabulary was jettisoned. A belief in social justice and a sense of the spiritual were seen to be mutually incompatible. This black-and-white perception can be put down in large measure to the callowness of youth. But I don't think that it is unfair to say that it also reflected the intellectual orthodoxies of the time. There is always a danger of becoming trapped permanently within the mode of thought fashionable in one's early twenties. It certainly took me a long time to accept the obvious—that there were some areas of life which reason could never comprehend or honor, which would turn to dust if approached analytically, but which could be honored in literature or in art generally—certain areas which could be better elucidated by rhyme than by reason.

It is no accident that we often turn to poetry at times of personal crisis— the break up of a love affair or the death of someone close to us. At its best, art engages us at several levels of our being, the physical and the emotional as well as the intellectual. So, when all is chaos on one level, there is sometimes a foothold or a handhold to be found somewhere else. Ultimately, and most starkly, there is the safety net of the *form* of tragedy which, terrible as it is, is preferable to a vision of utter chaos. In this sense, when I later came across the poems of Hölderlin and Rilke, Milosz and Levertov, I had a tremendous sense of having stumbled upon an entirely new vocabulary, of having somehow gained permission to think in directions in which I already felt, but had been censoring at an intellectual level. It is odd how, as post-Enlightenment philosophy found it more and more difficult to accommodate the idea of soul, soul somehow managed to find an uneasy refuge in art.

⁀

This was meant as a short essay on how I initially stumbled into poetry, having originally set off in quite another direction. It was when I returned to college in the early 1980s to study history again that I found myself finally thrown back upon language and what it offered. I felt that there was something extraordinarily brittle and short-lived about the truths yielded by historical research. It seemed to me that something was true only until fresh data became available or until its supporting ideology was supplanted by an alternative ideology. I found it exceedingly difficult to live with the implication that truth was relative and temporary. Again it was the *felt* evidence of language— something in the very *timbre* or timber of language, its rings of usage and growth —which offered some reassurance to the contrary. There was a truth in the resonance of certain words—bread, water, fire, love—evidence of a shared humanity, of shared need, shared desires, shared delight. (It is a truth which I often feel particularly in relation to the Irish language, precisely because, for better and for worse, the Irish language has survived on the periphery of European history. Although it has missed out on an enormous amount of its natural development, it has also escaped the fate of a number of European languages in having their core vocabulary purloined or held hostage for the purposes of political propaganda. Some sort of tenderness survives.)

I tried to articulate this, or rather to explain it to myself, in a number of poems which I wrote at about this time. In one of them, "Prodigal," I was asking language, tangible rather than abstract language, to rescue me from the corner into which I had backed myself:

Prodigal

Dark mutter tongue
rescue me,
I am drawn into outrageous worlds
where there is no pain or innocence,
only the little quiet sorrows
and the elegant joys of power.

Someone
businesslike in his desires,
has torn out the moon by its roots.
Oh, my tin king is down now mother

down and broken,
my clear browed king
who seemed to know no hungers
has killed himself.
Old gutter mother
I am bereft now,
my heart has learnt nothing
but the stab of its own hungers
and the murky truth of a half-obsolete language
that holds at least the resonance
of the throbbing, wandering earth.

Try to find me stones and mud now mother
give me somewhere to start,
green and struggling, a blade under snow,
for this place and age demand relentlessly
something I will never learn to give.

(Cannon 1990, 19)

Since the time of writing "Prodigal," twelve or thirteen years ago, language and stones have been very kind to me and have led me to many rich encounters. I can only ask that they continue to do so.

Medbh McGuckian. Photograph by Leon McAuley.
Courtesy of Wake Forest University Press.

Medbh McGuckian

Crystal Night

Our friends the enemy
gambled away eternity
for ten yards of wasteland,
a spout of soil where field
was laid unto field
below a street as wide
as the height of the houses.

For seven days yearly,
a murder timed to coincide
with the summer solstice,
they parade their boots, drums, songs,
their Unionist rhythms, insignia, flags,
their uniforms and pageantry,
their forests of banners,

their declarations of loyalty,
their endless repetitions of slogans,
their standard greetings,
their catechetical speeches,
their myopic, frustrated
ideology of the cheated
through the city of convulsionaries.

Prizing words only as fists,
or a series of insipid rosettes
that stand for protest.
At the chaste hour,
to appease the major-domos,
the ballet-masters danced
their choirs as if their columns
could conquer space.

As the earth is moved
from its position
by the weight of even a tiny bird
resting upon it,
so each gun moved into position
by nine tractors, required a crane
to insert each shell.

They would shoot high
if we would rearrange the earth
like the dust when a table
is struck. They would take care
to make their arms so encircling
pious and elegant
as melted down church bells

for a cannon to comb
a spider's web with its nailed
tongue, tearing his gliding
spinal cord from the cover
of his limbs,
that can never be bent
backwards or forwards.

And among all these injured things,
when the dwellers emerged slowly
to meet their liberators,

like a belated crowd
lost on a cricket pitch,
the goldfinch, its breast filled with lilies,
carried torch-downward, the spurge.

Rescuers and White Cloaks: Diary, 1968–69

It's 1968, over thirty years ago. I am seventeen, near the age of my eldest son. I have a Queen's University student diary of my brother's which he is not using and makes me feel more confident about passing the forthcoming entrance exams. But it is a world I do not know, a world of royalty and men. Under "Officers," the first title is "Visitor, Her Majesty the Queen." The Chancellor is Sir Tyrone Guthrie, whose house I will myself incredibly visit. Pro-chancellor is the Right Honourable Lord McDermott of Belmont, Lord Chief Justice. All are male, the President, the Treasurer, the Bursar, the Librarian. The Secretary is a man who shares with me now very kindly his retirement office. All the Deans of Faculties and all the Deans of Residence are masculine. My own religion comes at the end of a long bewildering list: Baptist, Brethren, Church of Ireland, Congregational, Jewish, Methodist, Non-Subscribing Presbyterian, Reformed Presbyterian. The Chaplain is now our parish bishop. The President of the Students' Union is Ciaran McKeown, who will run the Peace People—he does have a Lady Vice-President. Beside their names is an advert for dry-cleaning—"Men feel full of confidence in a perfectly laundered shirt." A shop selling typewriters and adding machines in Howard Street has evaporated along with its merchandise and half the street.

I have ticked only the Catholic Students' Society, little goody two-shoes. Not the Marxist Society nor the Campaign for Nuclear Disarmament, neither the Conservative and Unionist Association nor the Gaelic Drama Group. I hardly know what these are—the Independent Committee of One Hundred, the Labour Group and Independent Left, the Liberal Association, the National Democratic Group, the Steadfast Club, the Universal Club. As for culture, I never joined the Glee Club, the New Ireland Society, the Sixteen Club, the Tiddlywinks or Crucible Clubs, the Scottish Country Dancing Society, never mind International Relations. It must have all sounded like so much sex to me.

The terms are English terms—Michaelmas, Hilary, Trinity. There is an Air

Squadron and an Officer Training Corps. The railway is based at Queen's Quay and the only air service is BEA. A few restaurants open on Sunday, one Anglo-Chinese. There are three nighttime taxi firms for the whole city. At Ravenhill Rugby Pitch the Combined Provinces of Ireland play New Zealand in December. If you spend over thirty shillings at Pussy Boutique, you get 10 percent off sweaters. Men's shops have names like "Gay Lord" and "Oh Boy." There is still one called "Ideal Radio" and a "Gents' Hairdresser."

To hire skates at the King's Hall is one shilling. A letter costs 4d. and a parcel a half a crown. If I drink Pepsi I will come alive, the drink of my generation. St. Patrick's Day is not a holiday but Orangeman's Day is. The queen's birthday is a festival along with United Nations Day and the Conversion of St. Paul. As well there are conversion tables for furlongs and chains, pecks and bushels, all by permissions of H.M. Stationery Office. The First Aid advice is to lay the patient on *his* stomach, to remove your lips from the victim's face and allow *his* lungs to empty—a newly ironed handkerchief is usually fairly sterile on the inside.

Then my quotation from *Middlemarch*:

> To be a poet is to have a soul so quick to discern, that no shade of quality escapes it, and so quick to feel, that discernment is but a hand playing with finely ordered variety on the chords of emotion—a soul in which knowledge passes instantaneously into feeling and feeling flashes back as a new organ of knowledge. One may have that condition by fits only.
>
> (G. Eliot, 1997, 220)

1968
January

Cecil Day Lewis is the new Poet Laureate. I am in danger of falling in love with Ladislaw. Wore my mantilla to the evening Mass for World Poverty. There were blue orchids; I lit a red candle and said the rosary. My lips are sore and it is all the more painful because it seems a judgment for kissing. I discovered Wilfred Owen was homosexual. Read about Bob Dylan (Robert Zimmerman) in *Word*—he is twenty-seven and a poet. Keats and I no longer see eye to eye. I am sick to death of his sensuousness. Bloody battles in Saigon. I can see the poetry of medicine now. I stare at the moon like Meg Merrilies.[1]

---

1. An allusion to Keats's poem "Old Meg."

Charlotte Mew, "Sea Love":

> Tide be runnin' the great world over:
> 'Twas only last June month I mind that we
> Was thinkin' the toss and the call in the breast of the lover
> So everlastin' as the sea.
>
> Heer's the same little fishes that sputter and swim,
> Wi' the moon's old glim on the grey, wet sand;
> An' him no more to me nor me to him
> Than the wind goin' over my hand.
>
> (1953, 44)

February

I can't do my relative velocity questions. Saw "The Stress of Divorce"—how sad that a man should cry. I wonder what a pregnancy would be like. "Inquiry" was about women's rights. I saw the ice-skating on TV; the Russians were supremely beautiful—maybe I could make a poem out of their poetry. The sun spread its arms around the garden, and I waved at a helicopter. At school Martina had silver car polish on her nails. We had slides on the Passionist priests. Wordsworth on his own is bearable. I dreamt of an epic with everyone I know in it, rescuers and white cloaks. Also that my older sister was an unmarried mother. My younger sister became mature today. Is this the last part of growing up or a posthumous existence? Bobby Kennedy is standing.[2] It is winter in the morning and summer in the evening. I smelt a terrible smell everywhere all day—a sickly, putrid smell, as of death or sin. But it is gone now and the rain heals. I felt very dark and slept and slept like a woman's mouth.

Christina Rossetti, "Twice":

> As you set it down it broke—
> Broke, but I did not wince;
> At your judgment that I heard:
> But I have not often smiled
> Since then, nor questioned since,

2. Running for office.

Nor cared for corn-flowers wild,
Nor sung with the singing bird.
(1979, 125)

March

Should I call my love Hamlet or Porphyro? I need more images, not fewer. Red Alligator won the National, and Cambridge won the boat race. I began a poem in the orange lamplight, but the others came in. Some of the Beatles' lyrics, like "Lady Madonna," do show an awareness of poetry. I broke my rosary beads; the Vietnam War is being de-escalated. I don't see the dawn anymore going to school. But I walk tall and Camilla-like. I asked Mother how you could call on God if you didn't believe in Him, and she said the soul does on a supernatural level while the mind is confused on a natural level. I bought bias binding, but my body quivered so much I could not finish the pink dress. I saw a figure at the window and went to exposition—Good Friday—what is so good about it?

April

I had a dream last night about the woman who doesn't wear a hat in church and everyone was screaming and coming to see me in deputations. I felt like laughing all through the Stations of the Cross. No sadness during the cross. Even Wilfred Owen seemed cheerful by comparison—he must have been homosexual; it is all over the place. We went to see *The Song of Bernadette*. I don't come into the category for which no explanation is necessary nor that for which none is possible. The boy I met twice downtown in the raincoat with auburn hair has died of tetanus. I read Zhivago's poems. Princess Anne is beautiful even if she has got her driver's license. I went to mass almost as an afterthought. There was a boy with red mournful lips and eyes like wine. I have called him Malcolm. I read a poetry book by Elizabeth Jennings that made me feel ashamed and long to write, but I haven't the time yet. In the summer though, I shall dance! Ten golden leaves in my harvest hair. I went to a poetry reading in St. Malachy's Old Boys where the three poets gulped beer the whole time and struck me with disgust and envy. I loved "Childe Rowlande" the best.
    Edith Sitwell:

. . . the theme of the Gospel . . . proclaims Eternity as an event.—Barth: *The Epistle to the Romans*. Is not this true of the greatest poetry?

(1950, 158)

We must learn "to cram today with Eternity and not the next day." Kierkegaard: *Christian Discourses*.

(1950, 169)

May

He walked across the playground and my heart. I threw his love away, as bridegrooms do their wedding garments. English is very sour upon the tongue. Jane Austen can twist you around her little finger and then lightly flick you away to her other hand. There is something pure about this rain—it heals the fire in my throat. There was a grey-brown sunset. I dreamt I was modeling a red suit with a yellow blouse, my hair in blue ribbons. Everyone is sick of Owen but I pity him—the poetry is in the pity. Maybe I envy his fellowship, but he disturbs me. I lay in bed convulsive, like barbed wire in the breeze. I purged myself thus of my love with Chaucer, which now is alive in those words. My hair is a long brown river; my heart is doing complex harmonic motion. Am I a pantheist or simply touched? I saw him twice, once a silken prince, once as he was in the morning. Ovid is easy but dull. I feel the summer moving. I love beauty and I don't care what Owen says, poets aren't right just because they happen to be poets. Some say God caught them before they fell.

  T. S. Eliot, "Spleen":

> Sunday: this satisfied procession
> Of definite Sunday faces:
> Bonnets, silk hats and conscious graces
> In repetition that displaces
> Your mental self-possession
> By this unwanted digression.
>
> Evening, lights and tea!
> Children and cats in the alley;
> Dejection unable to rally
> Against this dull conspiracy.

And life, a little bald and grey,
Languid, fastidious and bland,
Waits, hats and gloves in hand,
Punctilious of tie and suit
(Somewhat impatient of delay)
On the doorstep of the Absolute.
(1969, 603)

June

There is a strange stillness, a shadow over everything. I am pale as a pined-for ghost. Soon. I dreamt of a red-and-white birth lately, of long fur staircases, and boys killed by bombs. Of orange spiders and buying stockings for a lesbian. Robert Kennedy was shot at midnight. At eight o'clock here. Anybody who has nerves, resign. What a long, deep day. When they told me Bobby was dead, I spilled ink all over myself. The sun made black blots on the road, cars were dusty. They played "Ave Verum" in St. Patrick's Cathedral for him. Sun poured out late in the evening. I hope he made his Easter Duty. I was too hopeful last week, thinking it was nearly over, when it has only begun. A smooth, sweet bath, I tossed all night, naked. Then dreamt of a deformed star, holy pictures. I am heart-stifled in my dell.

"The Three Ravens":

'Down in yonder greene field
There lies a knight spread under his shield;

His hounds they lie down at his feet,
So well do they their master keep;

'His hawks they fly so eagerly,
There's no fowl dare him come nigh.

'Down there comes a fallow doe,
As great with young as she might goe.

She lift up his bloudy head
And kist his wounds that were so red.

'She gat him upon her back,
And carried him to earthen lake.

'She buried him before the prime:
She was dead herself ere evensong time.
(Quiller-Couch 1924, 294)

July

My mother needn't say a novena—in the sixth month the angel came to a virgin. I am so afraid, as I fear children. The fire was small and humped. On me the summer storm and fever and melancholy wrought magic, as though I nothing was, which I like. I worried all night about my literary medium but Seamus will sort me out. I watched the death of the moon over the hill. Read *The Moon and Sixpence* by Somerset Maugham—colorsure, human, but not profound. Heavy white clouds with blue slits. We sat in the one-shilling-and-sixpence rows at the pictures. I washed my hair in milk flakes at great length. Dylan Thomas frightens me. The sunset was a crystal-clear wound. There was an immortal moth in the kitchen.

August, Ballycastle

There is awful poetry in me, I know, a small molten drip in a wet sea-cloud, but I cannot find it. My heart too small to hold its blood. I tried to put on makeup by candlelight—altarwise by owllight. Food tastes so alive here. Like heaven out of death, I watch the swirl of the sea with a lover's greed. *Warsaw Concerto*—peace—the Russians have invaded Czechoslovakia. Then I dreamt of gooseberry-shaped raspberries. A lamp lit as I passed it and I felt supremely me.
    Synge:

The poetry of exaltation will always be the highest, but when men lose their poetic feeling for ordinary life, and cannot write poetry of ordinary things, their exalted poetry is likely to lose its strength of exultation. . . . In these days poetry is usually a flower of evil or good, but it is the timber of poetry that wears most surely, and there is no timber that has not strong roots among the clay & worms. (1909, 1)

September

Persian earthquakes—sudden bursts of sun like yellow tulips. I sang like a lusty sparrow and was hailed blithe spirit. Edith Sitwell is rather too luscious and fairylike for my present state—maybe later. Read a bit about Hardy's love poems—"Bosinney," "Yeovil," religious differences, half a year between them. I could not wear that mask. I was crushed against a tall man. The sun went in dramatically. A boy with a feather said I had a beautiful face.

October

What is my right mind? Maybe I don't have one. My husband will be an artist, that's all I know. He phoned me at four after the march and let me caress his hand in the slide lecture—they were showing us the hands of Christ nailed by the wrists. The priest in Confession warned me to safeguard my purity—nothing could be easier. It was my first experience of both species; His blood was salty and sweet. We lost each other for the talk on atom bombs, but he sat at the end of my seat in the sex-talk. But we never touched each other; we tore it savagely to bits. I slammed out of the house before a letter could not arrive.

Austen, *Mansfield Park:*

> Fanny agreed to it, and had the pleasure of seeing him continue at the window with her, in spite of the expected glee; and having his eyes soon turned like hers towards the scene without.
>
> (1934, 113)

> Fanny had been everywhere awake to the difference of the country since February . . . the trees, though not fully clothed, were in that delightful state, when farther beauty is known to be at hand, and when, while much is actually given to the sight, more yet remains for the imagination.
>
> (1934, 446)

> She had not known before what pleasures she had to lose.
>
> (1934, 431)

November

Seamus in English class was flamboyantly high-and-mighty in purple and red. There was a bus protest to Stormont. A march and police all the way home. Nixon is president. He believed only in God. He wrapped his scarf around me as I said good-bye to him for the last time. My food hurt me, but the moon appeased me. I wondered if I had a vocation. A colored man passed me the salt—I am getting used to being the prey of men. I booked for "Room to Rhyme" and liked Seamus Heaney. But gave myself a beautiful headache and walked some of it away. November is a negative photograph, a dead dog buried in leaves.

Woolf, *To the Lighthouse*:

> She could be herself, by herself. And that was what she now often felt the need of—to think; well, not even to think. To be silent; to be alone. All the being and doing, expansive, glittering, vocal, evaporated; and one shrunk, with a sense of solemnity, into being oneself, a wedge-shaped core of darkness, something invisible to others. . . . Our apparitions, our external selves, were simply childish. Beneath, it was all dark, it was all spreading, it was unfathomably deep.
>
> (1997, 69)

Hopkins, "The Wreck of the Deutschland":

> Ah, touched in your bower of bone
> Are you! turned for an exquisite smart,
> Have you! make words break from me here all alone,
> Do you!—mother of being in me, heart.
>
> (1990, 123)

December

Alice and Granny outdid each other in eating nothing. After a lot of hints at staying, Alice was maneuvered out. I punned stupidly about Kant. Ann Savage is very tame. Patrick is growing a mustache and finding mice in girls' flats. Gold, sleek sunset, a hard sky where a star trembled occasionally—an extremely secular Christmas. I sewed a blue pillow slip. The astronauts are down safely. Brian let me carry out the legs of the record player. I hate that impossi-ble-to-read book, *Nostromo.*

Dylan Thomas, "From Love's First Fever to her Plague":

> And from the first declension of the flesh
> I learnt man's tongue to twist the shapes of thoughts
> Into the stony idiom of the brain,
> To shade and knit anew the patch of words
> Left by the dead who, in their moonless acre,
> Need no words' warmth.
>
> (1952, 21)

Dylan Thomas, "Out of Sighs":

> Were that enough, enough to ease the pain,
> Feeling regret when this is wasted
> That made me happy in the sun,
> How much was happy while it lasted,
> Were vagueness enough and the sweet lies plenty,
> The hollow words could bear all suffering
> And cure me of ills.
>
> (1952, 48)

1969
January

I don't know what to make of this P.D.[3] march. Frost and snow cover the world. Nora's New Year resolution must be to smile. I felt all clean inside and out, but laddered my extravagant blue tights. My slacks squeak. I could not recapture that party-love for him. His psychophantic methods awaken no spark in me. I should not have succumbed if I had not been intoxicated. I hope he doesn't phone. The kitchen was bright and silver at lunchtime—I felt sick with all the people passing. I went down to the library to consult books on pleasure and happiness. Aristotle seemed too dull and involved with the trees to have anything to do with beauty. I received the Host with joy and recogni-tion—make me innocent for him. His hair was like golden silk I twisted for his

---

3. People's Democracy, a political group.

sake. I adore hearing even his name. He always walks toward me when we meet; to hold his hand is a strange exploration. I have got so used to not being unloved, I am relearning to believe in God. Mr. Paisley had his march. My mother seemed carved out of wood.

Pound, "Near Perigord":

> She who could never live save through one person,
> She who could never speak save to one person,
> And all the rest of her a shifting change,
> A broken bundle of mirrors. . . !
>
> (1971, 157)

Donne, "Song":

> When thou sighest, thou sighest not winde
>   But sigh'st my soul away?
> When thou weep'st, unkindly kinde.
>   My life's blood doth decay.
>   It cannot bee
> That thou lov'st me, as thou say'st,
> If in thine my life thou waste,
>   Thou art the best of me.
>
>   (1991, 63)

February

It snowed all afternoon around my heart. The frost was like stars on the earth, the stars like frost in the sky. One pointing star like a nailhead. He said I wasn't patriotic and sang in Gaelic and asked me riddles. He was late because he had been too early. Winifred's hair glistened. She bound us together as before with her stained white coat. My poetry flows back in and out of me like a red stream. We did Eliot, and I was regal. I exaggerated the pain of my body to fit my soul's aridity. I knew he would dismiss my poem airily and treasure it within. I helped a man choose a valentine for his wife, and almost passed out against a lamppost. The trees were powdered alongside the Tech, like angels or lacework or fine crocheted gates. The snow fluttered with light like a sea-palace. I sounded thin and English on the tape recorder, as if I felt the stars pursuing me.

Yeats, "Owen Aherne and His Dancers":

> A strange thing surely that my heart,
> When love had come unsought,
> Upon the Norman upland or in that poplar shade,
> Should find no burden but itself and yet should be worn out.
> It could not bear that burden and therefore it went mad.
>
> The south wind brought it longing and the east wind despair,
> The west wind made it pitiful, and the north wind afraid.
> It feared to give its love a hurt with all the tempest there;
> It feared the love that he could give and therefore it went mad.
>
> I can exchange opinion with any neighbouring mind,
> I have as healthy flesh and blood as any rhymer's had.
> But O! my Heart could bear no more when the upland caught the wind;
> I ran, I ran, from my love's side because my Heart went mad.
>
> (1957, 449–50)

March

They read out of the Paschal letter on marriage and I put half-a-crown on the plate. The sun filled the Nativity window with roses. My mind is alive again to the power of words. A man on the bus started expounding on the Gospels and Abraham. I was too religious even to throw a snowball. The snowflakes were lazy parachutes and slow butterflies. One star dilated and died and was re-newed in the sable sky. Today was hung with shadows; my ashes were blue clay. English language is interesting until you try to learn it off. I was able to release some thoughts. 1984 is not a nightmare. The easiness of the exams seems unjust. I was almost late for psychology and then too early. We sat laughing hysterically in the Ladies' Common Room. How come I always love people on the phone and feel dubious about them in real life? I felt isolated when he spoke in Irish and said he'd been collecting for orphans all morning. But he talked politics in a way I could understand and of how he would right wrongs. I leaned my back on his breast. *The Rainbow* is a confused mass on which I shall force my own pattern. I hate the whole falseness of the elections. Mr. Paisley nearly beat O'Neill. I wanted to tear the air. He voted in my name. I am reserved in part of my heart and missed his look of communion, praising

God out of tune. Molly warned me with armpats. Though I gave him back his bracelet, I wouldn't change scarves again. (This is the last wild day of March.) Hemingway:

> If there were no war we would probably all be in bed. In bed I lay me down my head. Bed and board. Stiff as a board in bed. Catherine was in bed now between two sheets, over her and under her. Which side did she sleep on? Maybe she wasn't asleep. Maybe she was lying thinking about me. Blow, blow ye western wind. Well, it blew and it wasn't the small rain but the big rain down that rained. It rained all night. You knew it rained down that rained. Look at it. Christ, that my love were in my arms and I in my bed again. That my love Catherine. That my sweet love Catherine down might rain. Blow her again to me. Well, we were in it. Everyone was caught in it and the small rain would not quiet it.
>
> (1957, 204)

April

The lecture on MacNeice fitted with my yellow mood. He is too narrow in scope to mean very much and provides no answers. The sky full of dark blood running, the stars blue and gold fires. I feel a traitress no matter who I am with; I could not enter the sun. We had a long beautiful talk about nothing; he tossed my orange to pieces. My crowning glory is horrid, in the Latin sense. My work is shapeless and unattackable. The lamp dilated on the ceiling like a spinster; everyone had four eyebrows. I wish my poetry would come. Maybe prose would be better than poetry. People have no time nowadays. The whole secret is to be able to read fast—so said my esteemed faculty tutor. At the time I disagreed. Today was not in the least passionate. Too many people died in the film. Father Walsh said I had a great wee brain—there's an Irish lie for you. The streets were stark naked and stripped and openly ugly, a wasteland. My throat hurt after the fog, but the dawn was pastel as a shell, the sun feathered the trees, the wind tore blue holes. I was trembling with love and fright. My dreams were about nuclear war and American planes and a sense of silence. I dreamt of a thousand lost things and people. I remembered my schoolgirl devotion and that park with its breathing maiden promise. And resumed my lonely struggle with the mind.

My mother and I were intimate for a moment against men. Bruised white clouds, like a real face. Kant is so dry; I let my eyes devour him, do not read. My father removed the garden mound I loved to lean against. I can see death in his face. My nerves fired together all day, but I feel better after the poem. Cold cross buns. The nine Mass was said for the pope's intentions. I had two Holy Communions, but one was retrieved.[4] We fell in last year's leaves.

There is a sort of hot stillness which you can feel, and yet it is not hot nor is it still, but it will have you on edge and make you hot if you think about it. The feeling I always had for my father and it was in my brothers too.

May

Rain was dashing in nails against the window, and scudding in gold sparkles through blue air; the wind fell like fists. I had to do "Burnt Norton" without the book. I began *For Whom the Bell Tolls* and loved the rolling flow of it, so broad and vivid and strong after Woolf. I am avoiding myself and my imagination. My eyes feel blunt; I hated him while I loved his body. There have been post offices and reservoirs broken up and people hurt all weekend. Maybe a war would be good for us. Daddy's school was shut because of the water rations. One man, one vote has been barely passed; O'Neill is practically out. I feel incapable of being social, not having any superficiality, which is a necessary preliminary. I hate the academic approach to poetry. John says English here is sterile—maybe I will inseminate it.

Swinburne, "Before the Mirror":

> Face fallen and white throat lifted.
>> With sleepless eye
> She sees old loves that drifted,
>> She knew not why;
> Old loves and faded fears
> Float down a stream that hears
> The flowing of all men's tears beneath
>> the sky.
>
> (n.d., 58)

4. The priest took one host back.

Pound, "Fan-Piece, For Her Imperial Lord":

> O fan of white silk,
> clear as frost on the grass-blade,
> you also are laid aside.
>   (1971, 108)

June

A gold-white sky, the bus window was brown mist. The rain would rise, and then the sun would burn out. The leaves are so round and tough. Torrents of rain soothed the frozen soil of my mind; then the sky was steel blue like an old woman's face stretched with fear. At 9.15 there was a huge rolling crash like thunder, and the news said it was an orange and green flash. O'Neill has resigned. Daddy frightened me by predicting a United Europe. My mind feels charred and shaken like the new leaves. The secretary was like a duck, doubled up with pregnancy. Olive is unlike her name. I got sympathy from the radio, and saw outside a shop that Chichester-Clark had got in. I felt so weary and wretched with that woman kissing her third baby. The house seemed so grey, with the wind violating the virgin growth outside. The shadow and vanity of these days. I was in love with my body and now I detest it. Bent and battered over a table, I want to use language, not study it or how others use it. I want it alive in my mind. Stupid news about the Cabinet. I don't think I thought the whole day. I don't think I have really thought the whole year.

July

Martin let us read his poem: "The Frost-Bitten Man of Letters." I couldn't talk for not-being. Maybe some day I shall be writing about that, when he is dead and acclaimed. I can't imagine him serving Mass. I keep finding fault with English these days, like a mother with her child. Who am I to judge these pure creators? Not put-able into tidy boxes. 1984 just flowed past me in a dark tirade. He phoned with two-sixpences—his voice was thoroughly small and dry. The tulips were transparent; we plucked blossoms while we might. The tree outside spun lime greenly, the moon soft like a white cat. From now on I will be feminine to the death. Daddy had a £20 note. We didn't wear our best hats to mass. Colette was there in a black coat with freckles (not the coat, her). Sea shaded with blue and dark meeting trees. Gold moon on the horizon. Gabriel's poem: "To One I Almost Corrupted." I am Lesbia, a charming snake. Miss Aylward wanted to go to the fortune teller about her line.

Conrad Aiken, "Time in the Rock, Or Preludes to Definition":

> Disaster is no disaster on a starlit night.
> Look how the planets move. Look there, look there,
> How when the tree shakes the loosed star comes forth
> As impudent as ever! How can you keep
> Poor fool in such an angelic presence
> Your handful of pain? Look at that world
> So young, so fiery, so swift and so intent—
> And deny if you can that you too once
> Ran forth as splendidly as that. And how long since?
> Yesterday? This morning? Even as you look,
> That swift conviction burns once more—it is this instant:
> And all your life sums up one fiery thought,
> Bright as that loosed star, and begins again.
>
> (1970, 732–33)

August

A full peach-colored moon. He is not air to me. There were riots last night—my mind is filled with flowers and stains. A liquid gold dawn kneeling over the city. Trouble with the Apprentice boys in Derry, troops brought in. Five people dead last night. Troops in Belfast, in Ardoyne. We listened to the Athlone news. I sat reading Dante in a sunny interval, with white arrow-lines of cloud.

Sidney, *New Arcadia*:

> Night falls on one's shoulders like a judgment. Heretofore I have accused the sea, condemned the Pirates, and hated my evil fortune that deprived me of thee: but now thyself is the sea which drowns my comfort, thyself is the Pirate that robs thyself of me, thy own will becomes my evil fortune. (1987, 55).

Freedom dies at that point where man tries to bring his life into conformity with the visible, instead of the invisible.

(1987, 36)

September

We were on the Springfield Road, walking from Waterford Street to Bombay Street. I was shocked by the courage and spirit of the people, their sense not of outrage, but of frankness. The soldiers were demolishing the houses; there were many B-Specials. We went to Clonard Monastery, but he thinks tribunals a waste of time. We drove all around the barricades listening to Radio Ulster curbing Radio Free Belfast. There were news flashes about tear gas, a man shot dead this morning. It was half a loaf and a swift desperate kiss and my head on his shoulder—I hate to have him leave me, as if I wasn't part of his freedom.

Betjeman, "Death of King George V":

> Old men who never cheated, never doubted,
> Communicated monthly, sit and stare
> At the new suburb stretched beyond the run-way
> Where a young man lands hatless from the air.

(1958, 45)

October

I finished *Where Angels Fear to Tread*—stupid symbol of a book, nobody real in it. Two soldiers shot and Mrs. Keith's son got beaten up in Newington. But the barricades are down and we waved at the soldiers. Mass for Peace at 7.30; we prayed before the roses. After Dungiven we killed a seagull—I thought of Chekov. We had beautifying salads and Russian tea in the Abercorn. I had to pay 9d. on the bus. I read *The Writer's Craft*. More shooting last night, and after the riots the barricades are going up again. I dreamt I had three or four eyes. The dawn was a solid golden and rosy pearl. He carried the ciborium and was opaque-eyed with grief. My grandfather died October 21. The only brightness was the golden wood of the coffin. Wore my green jeans over to Queen's (poet!) and bought Jonson's *Comedies*. Two nice soldiers were searching cars. I went to Exposition, my parents to the Carmelites. I never felt warm with him, only peaceful, unbreathing.

November

We went to see *Love with the Proper Stranger.* It was what you might call "a night out." I am so glad I am not chained to a man's presence. I begin to get poetry back when I am free—is loneliness necessary for art? I saw the moon landing at eight. The pale music next door saddened me, made my womb hollow. I met Mary Green-eyeshadow; Miss Austria is Miss World.

December

I made my head sore with the Elizabethan sonnet. Huge explosion at about two—the petrol station down the road. Bernadette has got six months. He talked for three sixpences. I sent a Christmas-cum-birthday card to Dennis in Canberra. A dark skeletal hand spread across the blue—I dreamt of kissing a drowned baby and missing maxicoats in the sale.

Epilogue

Poetry Doesn't Pay

RITA ANN HIGGINS

People keep telling me
"Your poems, you know,
you've really got something there,
I mean really."

When the rent man calls, I go
down on my knees, and through
the conscience box I tell him,

This is somebody speaking,
short distance, did you know
I have something here with my poems?
People keep telling me.

"All I want is fourteen pounds
and ten pence, hold the poesy."

But don't you realize
I've got something here.

"If you don't come across
with fourteen pounds and ten pence soon

you'll have something at the side of the road,
made colourful by a little snow."

But.

"But nothing,
you can't pay me in poems or prayers
or with your husband's jokes,
or with photographs of your children
in lucky lemon sweaters
hand-made by your dead Grand Aunt
who had amnesia and the croup.

I'm from the Corporation,
what do we know or care about poesy,
much less grand amnostic dead aunts."

But people keep telling me.

"They lie.

If you don't have fourteen pounds
and ten pence, you have nothing
but the light of the penurious moon."
                                        (Higgins 1986, 20–21)

Works Cited

Index

Works Cited

Aiken, Conrad. 1970. *Collected Poems.* New York: Oxford Univ. Press.

Austen, Jane. 1934. *Mansfield Park.* London: Oxford Univ. Press.

Beresford, David. 1987. *Ten Dead Men: The Story of the 1981 Hunger Strike.* London: Grafton.

Berger, John. 1996. "Eleanor Wachtel Interviews John Berger." *Brick, A Literary Journal,* 53(winter):36.

Betjeman, John. 1958. *Collected Poems.* London: John Murray.

Boland, Eavan. 1967. *New Territory.* Dublin: Allen and Figgis.

———. 1975. *The War Horse.* London: Gollancz.

———. 1977. "Where Poetry Begins: An Interview with Eavan Boland." Conducted by Elizabeth Schmidt. *American Poet* (spring), 22–25.

———. 1980. *In Her Own Image.* Dublin: Arlen House.

———. 1982. *Night Feed.* Dublin: Arlen House. 1994. Manchester: Carcanet.

———. 1987. *The Journey.* Dublin: Arlen House; London: Carcanet.

———. 1990a. *A Kind of Scar: The Woman Poet in a National Tradition.* Dublin: Attic.

———. 1990b. *Outside History.* London: Carcanet.

———. 1990c. *Selected Poems.* Dublin: Arlen House; London: Carcanet.

———. 1991. *Outside History: Selected Poems 1980–1990.* New York: Norton.

———. 1994. *In a Time of Violence.* Manchester: Carcanet; New York: Norton.

———. 1995. *Object Lessons: The Life of the Woman and the Poet in Our Time.* Manchester: Carcanet; New York: Norton.

———. 1996. *An Origin Like Water: Collected Poems, 1967–1987.* New York: Norton.

———. 1997. *Anna Liffey.* Dublin: Poetry Ireland.

———. 1998. *The Lost Land: Poems.* Manchester: Carcanet; New York: Norton.

Brooks, Gwendolyn. 1963. *Selected Poems.* New York: Harper and Row.

Byron, Catherine, 1992a. *The Fat-Hen Hospital.* Bristol: Loxwood Stoneleigh.

———. 1992b. *Out of Step: Pursuing Seamus Heaney to Purgatory.* Bristol: Loxwood Stoneleigh.

———. 1993. *Settlements and Samhain.* Bristol: Loxwood Stoneleigh.

———. 2000. *The Getting of Vellum.* Co. Clare: Salmon.

Cannon, Moya. 1990. *Oar.* Galway: Salmon.

———. 1997. *The Parchment Boat.* Meath: Gallery.

Coughlan, Patricia. 1991. "Bog Queens: The Representations of Women in the Poetry of John Montague and Seamus Heaney." In *Gender in Irish Writing,* edited by Toni O'Brien Johnson and David Cairns, 88–111. Buckingham: Open Univ. Press.

Cunningham, John B. 1984. *Lough Derg: Legendary Pilgrimage.* Monaghan: n.p.

Curran, Patricia. 1989. *Grace Before Meals, Food Ritual and Body Discipline in Convent Culture.* Urbana: Univ. of Illinois Press.

Deane, Seamus, ed. 1991. *The Field Day Anthology of Irish Writing.* 3 vols. New York: Norton.

DeShazer, Mary. 1986. *Inspiring Women: Reimagining the Muse.* New York: Pergamon.

Dillard, Annie. 1976. *Pilgrim at Tinker Creek.* London: Picador.

Dillon, Eilís. 1980. "The Lament for Arthur O'Leary." *In Soft Day; A Miscellany of Contemporary Irish Writing,* edited by Peter Fallon and Sean Golden, 36–48. South Bend, Ind.: Univ. of Notre Dame Press.

Donne, John. 1991. *John Donne: The Complete English Poems.* Edited by David Campbell. London: Everyman's Library.

Elgin, Suzette Haden. 1987. *The Judas Rose.* New York: Daw.

Eliot, George. 1997. *Middlemarch.* London: Oxford Univ. Press.

Eliot, T. S. 1969. *The Complete Poems and Plays of T. S. Eliot.* London: Faber and Faber.

Ellmann, Maud. 1993. *The Hunger Artists.* London: Virago.

García Lorca, Federico. 1960. *Selected Poems: A Bi-lingual Edition.* Harmondsworth: Penguin.

Gordon, Lyndall. 1977. *Eliot's Early Years.* New York: Oxford Univ. Press.

———. 1988. *Eliot's New Life.* New York: Oxford Univ. Press.

Hall, Donald. 1962. *Contemporary American Poetry.* Harmondsworth: Penguin.

Hartigan, Anne Le Marquand. 1996. *Clearing the Space: A Why of Writing.* Galway: Salmon.

Heaney, Seamus. 1966. *Death of a Naturalist.* London: Faber and Faber.

———. 1984. *Station Island.* London: Faber and Faber.

———. 1988. *The Government of the Tongue, Selected Prose 1978–87.* London: Faber and Faber.

Hemingway, Ernest. 1957. *A Farewell to Arms*. New York: Scribner's.

Higgins, Rita Ann. 1986. *Goddess & Witch*. Galway: Salmon

Hopkins, Gerard Manley. 1990. *The Poetical Works of Gerard Manley Hopkins*. Edited by Norman MacKenzie. Oxford Univ. Press.

Hyde, Douglas. [1904]. 1971. *The Love Songs of Connaught*. Reprint. Shannon: Irish Univ. Press.

Kavanagh, Patrick. 1964. *Self-Portrait*. Dublin: Dolmen.

Kinnell, Galway. 1974. *The Avenue Bearing the Initial of Christ into the New World*. Boston: Houghton Mifflin.

Larkin, Philip. 1964. *Whitsun Weddings*. London: Faber and Faber.

MacNeice, Louis. 1949. *Collected Poems, 1925–48*. London: Faber and Faber.

McGuckian, Medbh. 1980a. *Portrait of Joanna*. Belfast: Ulsterman Publications.

———. 1980b. *Single Ladies*. Devon: Interim.

———. 1982. *The Flower Master*. Oxford: Oxford Univ. Press.

———. 1984. *Venus and the Rain*. Oxford: Oxford Univ. Press. 1993. (Rev. ed., Meath: Gallery; Winston-Salem: Wake Forest Univ. Press, 1994.)

———. 1988. *On Ballycastle Beach*. Oxford: Oxford Univ. Press; Winston-Salem: Wake Forest Univ. Press. (Rev. ed., Meath: Gallery, 1995.)

———. 1991. *Marconi's Cottage*. Meath: Gallery. (Reprint, Winston-Salem: Wake Forest Univ. Press, 1992.)

———. 1993. *The Flower Master and Other Poems*. Meath: Gallery.

———. 1994. *Captain Lavender*. Meath: Gallery. (Reprint, Winston-Salem: Wake Forest Univ. Press, 1995.)

———. 1997. *Selected Poems 1978–1994*. Meath: Gallery; Winston-Salem: Wake Forest Univ. Press.

———. 1998. *Shelmalier*. Meath: Gallery.

Meehan, Paula. 1994. *Pillow Talk*. Meath: Gallery.

Mew, Charlotte. 1953. *Collected Poems*. London: Gerald Duckworth.

Milligan, Alice. 1993. *The Harper of the Only God*. Edited by Sheila Turner Johnston. Omagh, Co. Tyrone: Colourpoint Press.

Mills, Lia. 1995. " 'I Won't Go Back to It': Irish Women Poets and the Iconic Female." *Feminist Review* 50: 69–88.

Monson, Craig, A., ed. 1992. *The Crannied Wall: Religion and the Arts in Early Modern Europe*. Ann Arbor: Univ. of Michigan Press.

Montague, John. 1989. *The Rough Field*. Meath: Gallery.

———, ed. 1974. *The Faber Book of Irish Verse*. London: Faber and Faber.

Morash, Chris, ed. 1995. *Creativity and Its Contexts*. Dublin: Lilliput.

Murphy, Richard. 1963. *Sailing to an Island*. London: Faber and Faber.

Muske, Carol. 1997. *Women and Poetry: Truth, Autobiogrphy and the Shape of the Self*. Ann Arbor: Univ. of Michigan Press.

Neruda, Pablo. 1970. *Selected Poems:* Edited by Nathaniel Tarn. London: Jonathan Cape.

———. *1972. The Captain's Verses.* New York: New Directions.

Newmann, Joan. 1994. *Circumcision Party.* Belfast: HU Publications.

———. 1995. *Coming of Age.* Belfast: Blackstaff.

———. 1998. *Thin Ice.* Belfast: Abbey Press.

Ní Chuilleanáin, Eiléan. 1972. *Acts and Monuments.* Dublin: Gallery.

———. 1975. *Site of Ambush.* Dublin: Gallery.

———. 1981. *The Rose-Geranium.* Dublin: Gallery.

———. 1985. *Irish Women: Image and Achievement.* Dublin: Arlen House.

———. 1986. *The Second Voyage.* Dublin: Gallery; Newcastle upon Tyne: Bloodaxe Books. 1991. (Rev. ed. Winston-Salem: Wake Forest Univ. Press.)

———. 1989. *The Magdalene Sermon.* Meath: Gallery.

———. 1991. *The Magdalene Sermon and Earlier Poems.* Winston-Salem: Wake Forest Univ. Press.

———. 1994. *The Brazen Serpent.* Meath: Gallery.

Ní Dhomhnaill, Nuala. 1981. *An Dealg Droighin.* Corcaigh: Clo Mercier.

———. 1984. *Féar Suaithinseach.* Ma Nuat: An Sagart.

———. 1988. *Selected Poems: Rogha Dánta.* Dual language text translated by Michael Hartnett. Dublin: Raven Arts. (Reprint, Dublin: New Island Books, 1993.)

———. 1990. *Pharaoh's Daughter.* Dual language text with many translators. Meath: Gallery.

———. 1992. *The Astrakhan Cloak.* Poems in Irish. Translations by Paul Muldoon. Meath: Gallery. (Reprint, Winston-Salem: Wake Forest Univ. Press, 1993.)

Ní Dhuibhne, Eilís. 1995. *Voices on the Wind; Women Poets of the Celtic Twilight.* Dublin: New Island Books.

O'Brien, Kate. [1941]. 1988. *The Land of Spices.* London: Virago.

O'Brien, Peggy. 1992–93. "Lough Derg, Europe and Seamus Heaney." *Irish University Review* 13 (winter): 122–30.

O'Faolain, Sean. 1981. "Lovers of the Lake." *The Heat of the Sun.* Harmondsworth: Penguin.

O'Malley, Mary. 1990. *A Consideration of Silk.* Galway: Salmon.

———. 1993. *Where the Rocks Float.* Galway: Salmon.

———. 1997. *The Knife in the Wave.* Galway: Salmon.

———. 2001. *Asylum Road.* Co. Clare: Salmon.

Ong, Walter. 1971. *Rhetoric, Romance and Technology.* Ithaca: Cornell Univ. Press.

Pound, Ezra. 1971. *Personae: The Collected Shorter Poems of Ezra Pound.* New York: New Directions.

Quiller-Couch, Arthur, ed. 1924. *The Oxford Book of Ballads.* London: Oxford Univ. Press.

Raine, Kathleen. 1967. *Defending Ancient Springs*. London: Oxford Univ. Press.

Rich, Adrienne. 1979. "When We Dead Awaken: Writing as Revision." In *On Lies, Secrets and Silence, Selected Prose 1966–78,* 33–49. New York: Norton.

———. 1993. *What Is Found There: Notebooks on Poetry and Poetics*. New York: Norton.

Roethke, Theodore. 1972. "The Poet's Business." In *Straw for the Fire: The Notebooks of Theodore Roethke, 1943–63,* edited by David Wagoner, 170–79. Garden City, New York: Doubleday.

Rose, Gillian. 1995. *Love's Work*. London: Chatto and Windus.

Rossetti, Christina. 1979. *The Complete Poems*. Edited by R. W. Crump. Baton Rouge: Louisiana Univ. Press.

Sidney, Philip. 1987. *The Countess of Pembroke's Arcadia (The New Arcadia)*. Edited by Victor Skretkowicz. Oxford: Clarendon.

Sitwell, Edith. 1950. *A Poet's Notebook*. Boston: Little, Brown.

Stevens, Wallace. 1955. "Thirteen Ways of Looking at a Blackbird." In *Collected Poems*. London: Faber and Faber.

Strong, Eithne. 1961. *Songs of Living*. Monkstown: Runa.

———. 1974. *Sarah, in Passing*. Dublin: Dolmen.

———. 1980, 1993. *Flesh . . . the Greatest Sin*. Monkstown: Runa; Dublin: Attic.

———. 1985. *My Darling Neighbour*. Donnybrook: Beaver Row.

———. 1993. *Spatial Nosing: New and Selected Poems*. Swords: Poolbeg/Salmon.

Swinburne, Algernon Charles. n.d. *Swinburne's Selected Poems*. Philadelphia: David MacKay.

Synge, John. 1909. *Poems and Translations*. Dundrum: Cuala.

Thomas, Dylan. 1952. *Collected Poems*. London: J. M. Dent.

Thomson, George. 1988. *Island Home: The Blasket Heritage*. Kerry: Brandon.

Watts, Carol. 1992. "Releasing Possibility into Form; Cultural Choice and the Woman Writer." In *New Feminist Discourses,* edited by Isobel Armstrong, 83–102. London: Routledge.

Woolf, Virginia. 1997. *To the Lighthouse*. London: Penguin.

Yeats, William Butler. 1957. *Variorum Edition of the Poems of W. B. Yeats*. Edited by Peter Allt and Colonel Alspach. New York: Macmillan.

———. [1936] 1968. "Modern Poetry: A Broadcast." In *Yeats: Essays and Introductions,* 491–508. New York: Macmillan.

Yogananda, Paramahansa. 1993. *The Autobiography of a Yogi*. 12th ed. Los Angeles: Self-Realization Fellowship.

Index